TERRORISM
AND
COUNTERTERRORISM

TERRORISM AND COUNTERTERRORISM

Editor

Dr. Vijay Khare

Foreword by

Prof. (Dr.) Nitin R. Karmalkar

Vice Chancellor, Savitribai Phule Pune University
(formerly University of Pune) Ganeshkhind, Pune-411007. India.

PENTAGON PRESS LLP

Terrorism and Counterterrorism
Editor: Dr. Vijay Khare

First Published in 2019

ISBN 978-93-86618-71-9

Disclaimer: The views expressed in this volume are of individual contributors and do not represent the viewpoint of the editor or publisher.

Published by
PENTAGON PRESS LLP
206, Peacock Lane, Shahpur Jat
New Delhi-110049
Phones: 011-64706243, 26491568
Telefax: 011-26490600
email: rajan@pentagonpress.in
website: www.pentagonpress.in

Printed at Aegean Offset Printers, Greater Noida, U.P.

For the younger generation of scholars

of

Defence and Strategic Studies

Contents

Savitribai Phule Pune University
(formerly University of Pune)
Ganeshkhind, Pune-411007, India.

Telephone: 020-25693868
Fax: 020-25693233
E-mail: puvc@unipune.ac.in

Prof. (Dr.) Nitin R. Karmalkar
Vice Chancellor

FOREWORD

Dr. Vijay Khare has, with his book Terrorism and Counter-terrorism, provided an indispensible contribution to Defence and Strategic Studies. This book is a modest effort to analyze and reflect upon the diverse challenges of terrorism faced by the world. It deals with various facets of terrorism and counter-terrorism, which are debatable between researchers, academicians and policy makers. It not only contributes to the concept of emerging challenges of terrorism policy makers but also of terrorism and its social, economical, political and physiological impact on human being. This volume vividly covers diverse aspects of terrorism and internal security issues such as military power, counter-terrorism and mechanism, radicalization and violent extremism, insurgency, low intensity conflicts and internal security issues. It enriches students, researchers and policy makers with abundant empirical evidence to bring forth the significance of various challenges and possible responses.

Dr. Khare asserted that contemporary terrorism is hologrammatic: it thrives on fear emanated through violence and propagated by using communication technology. It has tweaked the traditional concept of security and shifted the entire debate to a non-traditional security domain. In order to launch effective counter-terrorism measures, it requires strategic centre focused on human security and national interest. In most of the counter-terrorism strategies, the role of law enforcement agency and domestic intelligence has drastically increased.

I would like to congratulate Dr. Vijay Khare, Professor and Head, Department of Defence and Strategic Studies (DDSS), Yashwantrao Chavan National Centre of International Security and Defence Analysis (YC-NISDA) and Strategic Culture and Security Foundation for an impeccable piece of work and wish them all the very best for their endeavours ahead and hope that DDSS, YC-NISDA will bring more laurels to Savitribai Phule Pune University.

Prof. (Dr.) Nitin R. Karmalkar

Preface

The book focuses on contemporary problem faced by the world – Terrorism. Terrorism is a very complex term to be defined because of the lack of clarity in the manifestations of terrorist acts, motives and their objectives. Primarily, terrorism is often referred to as an act of violence directed towards civilians and non-combatants in pursuit of political or ideological aim. Today, terrorism has become one of the biggest security challenges to world community. It can threaten the dignity and security of human beings to a great extent; disturb peaceful existence and create fear in the minds of people and also jeopardize the very fundamental freedom and destabilize governments.

The present work is primarily a result of an International Seminar on Terrorism and Counter-terrorism organized by the Department of Defence & Strategic Studies (DDSS) and Yashwantrao Chavan National Center of International Security and Defence Analysis (YC-NISDA). I would like to thank the Indian Council of Social Science Research (ICSSR) for their support and providing funds to organize the international seminar.

I express my deep gratitude to the Hon'ble Professor Nitin R. Karmalkar, Vice-Chancellor, SPPU, for writing the 'Foreword' of the book.

Contemporary terrorism is hologrammatic; it thrives on fear emanated through violence and propagated by using communications technology. Contemporary terrorism has shaken the traditional concept of security. It has shifted the entire debate to a non-traditional security domain. To carry out effective counter-terrorism measures, it requires a strategic centre focused on human security and national interest. In most of the counter-terrorism strategies, the role of law enforcement agency and domestic intelligence has drastically increased.

The book has eleven articles; each article gives a vivid insight on terrorism and counter-terrorism strategy/policy. Professor Scott Gartner talks about The

Victory Trap and how easy win becomes a costly affair of sustenance. He has constructed a debate around weak states, strong states and failed states. Mr. Shrinivasrao S. Sohoni believes that radicalization and violent extremism which are burgeoning as incalculably potent are threats to national security. He has given very informative and cognitive list of recommendations towards containing and countering the twin menaces. Professor Dilip Mohite gives a broad and realistic perspective of terrorism. He opines India faces the issue of terrorism/insurgency which is directly threatening security, welfare and integrity. Lt Gen (Retd.) DB Shekatkar explained about the terrorism: Counter Challenges and Military Power. Prof. Tridip Chakraborty explains the saga of insurgency, low-intensity conflicts and terrorism in Southeast Asia with special focus on ASEAN's riposte on counter-terrorism.

Nitin A Gokhale examines the internal armed conflicts through the eyes of terrorism and insurgency. International disturbances – terrorism, civil disturbances, subversion, insurgency and civil war – pose a threat, varyingly to law and order, public order and/or the security of the state. Dr. Sushama Bhosale brings out psychological connection of terrorism. She has argued that psychological tool can mitigate terrorist attack. It is possible to deradicalisation the youth, prevent them from pursuing such heinous acts.

Air Marshal Bhushan Gokhale's article vividly covers various aspects of terrorism and internal security issues such as military power, counter-terrorism mechanism, insurgency, low intensity conflicts and internal securities issues. Dr. Arun Vishwanathan has tackled the greatest fear of terrorism, i.e., nuclear attack. He has focused on the historical progress of nuclear security debate and gives possible nuclear terrorism scenario. In conclusion, he argues that as terrorist groups continue to adopt innovative means of carrying out attacks and make growing use of technology in such attacks, it becomes imperative to employ a 'system-approach' to security to prevent nuclear material and technology from falling in the hands of terror groups. Brig. Madhusudan R. Mutatkar focused on the military diplomacy. In the article, he analysis the Chinese model and suggests some conclusions to be drawn by India.

I am very fortunate in having received enthusiastic and overwhelming contribution from the esteemed authors and academicians. I feel it's my duty to express my gratitude to all those who have wholeheartedly supported this book , especially my research team: Dr. Ankur Yadav, Dr. Ravi Thorat, PJ Khache, Sandip Javir, Dnyaneshwar Gaikwad, Sheetal Jagtap, Ganesh, Mr. Gadadare, Dr. Dimpal Chaudhary, Bharati Kokil, Raisa Choudhury, Vijay

Mohad and Gaurav Kokil for their support. As there are less number of publications dedicated to this particular topic, I feel that we have filled that void for the students, researchers and policy makers. The book will bridge the gap between the researchers and academicians on one hand and officers and general public on the other hand.

I am thankful for the publishers for bringing out the book within the shortest possible time. I hope that the readers will find our efforts worthy and the book will serve the expected needs.

Dr. Vijay Khare
Dean, Faculty of Humanities
Professor & Head, Department of Defence & Strategic Studies
Savitribai Phule Pune University

About the Contributors

Dr. Scott Sigmund Gartner is the Director of the Penn State School of International Affairs and Professor of International Affairs, Department of Political Science (affiliate), the School of Law (affiliate) and the Engineering Systems Program (affiliate). Professor Gartner's research focuses on national and international security, counter-terrorism, cyber security, international conflict mediation and policy assessment. Gartner teaches classes in national security, conflict management, international affairs, foreign policy and research design. Prior to joining Penn State, he directed the International Relations Program at the University of California Davis, where he was a Professor of Political Science.

Professor Gartner's over fifty academic publications includes books such as *Strategic Assessment in War*, *International Conflict Mediation: New Approaches and Findings* and *The Historical Statistics of the United States*, in addition to articles in top journals in political science, sociology, international affairs, history, military intelligence, public policy, international negotiations, and communications. His honors include the Jefferson award for the best government resource, the RUSA Outstanding Reference Award, Booklist Editor's Choice Award, Library Journal Best Reference Award, History News Network Book of the Month and the American Political Science Association's best policy thesis award. Gartner's research has been funded by the National Science Foundation, the National Security Administration, The National Counter Terrorism Center, the Folke Bernadotte Academy, and the Sloan foundation. He is currently working on studies of 1) counter terrorism, 2) military casualties and politics, 3) international dispute mediation and 4) suicide in the military.

Shrinivasrao S. Sohoni is a Governance Specialist and Strategic Analyst., Mr Sohoni entered the Indian Administrative Service in 1970 after his education at The Doon School, Dehra Dun, and St. Stephen's College, Delhi. His key assignments were in the Government of India in the Department of Cabinet Affairs, Union Cabinet Secretariat, the Ministry of Defence, the Ministry of Industry, Parliament, and in India's neighborhood.

During a period of endemic political turbulence in the country, and four changes of government at the Centre, Mr. Sohoni was Secretary to the President of India, and Secretary-General of the Rajya Sabha, having previously served as Additional Secretary in the President's Secretariat and of the Rajya Sabha, and Secretary to the Governor of Maharashtra.

Through 2006 to 2014, Mr Sohoni served as Senior Adviser in the Office of the President of the Islamic Republic of Afghanistan, — advising the Afghan President and mentoring the young Cabinet Secretary and senior officials in the President's Secretariat on a range of governance issues including, especially, subjects germane to Afghanistan's Constitutional, Political, and National Security perspectives. A student of Comparative Religion, especially Islam, history of Islam, and connected trends and entities, Mr. Sohoni's current focus is on the problem of Islamic Terrorism and Extremism, and the organization of State and Civil Society approaches for purposes of Counter-Terrorism/ Extremism.

Prof Dilip Mohite, Former Professor and Head, Coordinator for Ford-Foundation Programme in International Relations and DSA Programme, Department of Political Science, Faculty of Arts, M S University of Baroda. He also held the position of the Dean, Faculty of Arts, the M S University of Baroda. Professor Mohite earned his Ph.D. from University of Mumbai and pursued a post-doctoral research at the Fletcher School of Law and Diplomacy, Tufts University, USA. He was a Senior Fulbright Fellow at the Stimson Center, Washington as well as a Fellow at the University of Wisconsin, Madison and German Academic Council. He was the President's Nominee at the Jawaharlal Nehru University between 2010 and 2015. He has been a Visiting Faculty at the University of Mumbai and Savitribai Phule Pune University. He has been on the UGC Advisory Committees at several universities. He has held the positions of General Secretary and President of the Indian Association of American Studies. Professor Mohite has published several books and articles, and has organized several international and national conferences and seminars.

Lt Gen Dr D B Shekatkar is the President of Forum for integrated National Security. He chaired Committee of Experts (Shekatkar Committee) constituted by Ministry of Defence Government of India to recommend measures to enhance defence capability and optimise defence expenditure of the armed forces. Gen Shekatkar retired as Director General of Indian Army's Perspective Planning. He held an important appointment of Commandant of Infantry School & College, MHOW during his Army tenure. Dr Shekatkar was part of the Indian delegation responsible for negotiations with China about Indo-China border dispute.

Dr. Tridib Chakraborti is a Professor and Ex-Head of the Department of International Relations, Jadavpur University, Kolkata. He is an expert of South, Southeast Asian and Asia Pacific affairs, *Indian Political Thought and Foreign Policy and Strategic Studies.* He has written more than 46 articles on different topics related to Southeast and South Asia in edited volumes, published by Routledge (London), Frontpage Publications (London), Malaysian Centre for Ethnic Studies, Selangor, Malaysia, Institute of South East Asian Studies Publications (Singapore), Concept Publisher, Shipra Publications, Pentagon Press, New Century Publications, Pearson, Knowledge World Publishers, Gyan, Monahar, Allied Publisher, RIS of New Delhi, etc. His first book was *India and Kampuchea: A phase in their Relations – 1978-81* (Minerva Associates (Publications) Pvt. Ltd. Kolkata, 1985. He has also co-edited seven books on International Relations. Besides this, he is a regular contributor of articles in internationally and nationally reputed journals. He travels abroad frequently to deliver lectures and attend seminars and conferences. In 2015, he has been selected as a visiting Professor of ICCR Chair at Dublin City University, Dublin, Ireland.

Nitin A Gokhale, South Asia's leading strategic analysts, , a veteran journalist with 31 years experience across web, print and broadcast mediums, he keeps himself busy with writing, lecturing and making documentaries. An authoritative defence analyst, media trainer and a multi-media reporter who started his career in 1983, he has the rare distinction of living and reporting from India's North-eastern region for 23 years. In his distinguished journalism career, he has reported the Kargil War, the Eelam War IV in Sri Lanka for three years and different insurgencies from Kashmir, North-east and Maoist-hit areas and has worked with as diverse media houses as The Telegraph, Sunday, Outlook, Tehelka and NDTV. Over the past decade he has specialised in reporting and analysing India-China relations and has extensively travelled in Tibet, Ladakh, Arunachal Pradesh and China.

Author of four books on insurgency, war, military and demography, he regularly teaches and lectures at India's National Defence College, the Army, Navy and Air Force War Colleges, Defence Services Staff College, the Indian Institute of Mass Communication, the Intelligence Bureau's Training School and the College of Defence Management. A keen student of India's neighbourhood and its strategic space, he has moved on from full-time journalism in December 2014 to pursue his book writing projects, conducting training in media handling and penning columns in print and web.

Dr. Sushama Bhosale is the Head & Associate Professor of Psychology, Annasaheb Magar College, Affiliated to Savitribai Phule Pune University. She has work experience of about 20 years. She completed her Ph.D. in Psychology from Savitribai Phule Pune University. Dr. Sushama Bhosale has delivered more than three hundred speech to various government and non government organizations. She is a member of various national and international bodies related to Psychology. She is also a member of various university bodies. She has extended her consultancy to national and international students related to their psychological problems. Every year various programmes are organized by her for the mentally disabled children.

Air Marshal Bhushan Gokhale was commissioned into the Indian Air Force in June 1968 in fighter stream and has seen active operations during the 1971 Indo-Pak hostilities on both Eastern and Western fronts. He has served as Flying Instructor in Iraq from 1977 to 1979 and as the Defence Adviser at Indian Embassy in Egypt from 1994 to 1998. He is a graduate of the Defence Services Staff College and is M.Sc., M.Phil. from Madras University. He is also an alumnus of the Air War College, USA and Fellow of Aeronautical Society of India. He was the Vice Chief of Air Staff at Air Headquarters prior to his retirement on 31st December, 2007. During service he was awarded PVSM, AVSM and VM.

On retirement, Air Marshal Gokhale has been appointed Consultant to the Principle Scientific Advisor to the GOI and also to DRDO. For his post retirement contribution in the Indigenous development of Strategic systems he was awarded the prestigious Agni award on the National Technology Day 2013. In May 2010, he was detailed as the Chairman with full judicial powers, to investigate into the tragic Air India Express accident at Mangalore.

Dr. Arun Vishwanathan is Assistant Professor, Department of Defence and Strategic Studies, Savitribai Phule Pune University. He has held the position of Assistant Professor, National Institute of Advanced Studies (NIAS), Bangalore and Assistant Director, National Security Council Secretariat (NSCS). Arun holds a doctorate in International Relations from Jawaharlal Nehru University. His specialisation is on nuclear deterrence and strategy, nuclear weapons and missile capabilities in India's neighbourhood and export controls. Arun has co-edited a book *Troubling Tehran: Reflections on Geopolitics* and contributed to journals like *Strategic Analysis, Contemporary Review of Middle East, USI Journal, Indian Foreign Affairs Journal, Synergy: CENJOWS Journal* in addition to several articles in the media and online publications. He is an elected Member of the International Institute of Strategic Studies (IISS), London and Associate Member of the United Service Institution of India (USI) and the Institute of Defence Studies and Analysis (IDSA), New Delhi.

Brig Mutatkar M Ramchandra was commissioned to the Mahar Regiment in 1986 and was first posted to the sensitive Indo-Tibet border. The officer has vast experience of serving in active counter insurgency and Line of Control environment in Jammu & Kashmir, for over a decade, during Operations Rakshak & Parakramand later in Nagaland and Mizoram during Operation Orchid. In 1997 he was selected to join a new battalion of Jammu & Kashmir Light Infantry; and subsequently, he raised a new Assam Rifle Battalion in the North-East sector on the Indo-Myanmar border. During the Higher Command Course at Army War College, Mhow, his dissertation on "China's Economic and Military Engagement with India's neighbours and its implications" was selected for publication in the War College Journal of Spring 2009. During the National Conference on India-China Relations held in SPPU in February 2018, he presented a paper on "Military Diplomacy: Analysis of the Chinese model and Lessons for India". He recently completed a Resident Scholar Programme with the SPPU (Pune University) from 2016 to 2018 with the research subject – "China's Military Diplomacy; Analysis of China's Military Outreach".

1

Defining Terrorism and Counterterrorism at the Global Stage

Prof Vijay Khare

The statement, "One man's terrorist is another man's freedom fighter", started a new debate in terrorist literature.[1] Terrorism is not a new concept, and has been used very often over the past decades. It is one of the most difficult terms to define, and a debatable one. Any definition of terrorism includes different debates.[2] For example, Schmidt and Jongman, in their book, *Political Terrorism*, mentioned 109 different definitions of terrorism.[3] Although the definitions of terrorism vary widely, all come from a common point: terrorism is an act of unlawful use of violence and intimidation, especially against civilians, in the pursuit of political aims. It means pre-meditated and politically motivated violence perpetrated against non-combatant targets by sub-national groups or clandestine agents, usually intended to influence citizens.

Traditional Classification and New Classification

In the 1880s, an initial "Anarchist Wave" appeared which continued for some 40 years. Its successor, the "Anti-Colonial Wave" began in the 1920s, and by the 1960s had largely disappeared. The late 1960s witnessed the birth of the "New Left Wave," which dissipated largely in the 1990s leaving a few groups still active in Sri Lanka, Spain, France, Peru, and Columbia. The fourth "Religious Wave" began in 1979, and, if it follows the pattern of its predecessors, it still has twenty to 25 years to run.

The classification of subjects of terror could be built on the basis of the raveling definitions. In general the characteristics also indicated the profound connotation, the main motivation. Even the political nature of the subject identified has finally entered a new phase of transition, for example, the terrorist attack typology after the train explosion in Madrid and other parts of the world. Therefore, the terrorists identify on the basis of their motivation to act and identify on the basis of their politic. The criteria for distinction were mainly three:

1. Political statements such as terrorist demand.
2. The political connotation of terrorists
3. The regions they belong to, politically and geographically, etc.

Old and New Terrorism

For analysing the difference between old and new terrorism, three key aspects can be debated as goals, methods and organisations. The ideology of traditional or old terrorism being a political weapon is to maintain a regime, or to create the conditions for a new one. The old terrorism is more comprehensible, limited and more specific with roots in political ideology.[4] It is homegrown and has consequences for the nation, its institutions, population, property and policies. The victims, perpetrators and audience are all from same country. According to Walter, the old domestic terrorism, states were self-reliant if they possessed sufficient resources. Therefore, antiterrorist strategies did not involve other states, as neither the terrorist acts nor the government's reactions affected foreign interests.[5]

The new terrorism is appropriately defined and its applicability to current circumstances is evaluated. New terrorism targets to kill as many as possible. The 9/11 terrorist attacks have totally transformed the perception of terrorism throughout the world and required redefining a long list of concerns regarding international and national security.[6] The new terrorism was justified on a religious base. The new terrorist group has an ambiguous goal on the systemic level. According to Stephane Leman, a transnational terrorist organisation is based in one country but operates at times outside its territory. An international terrorist organisation not only operates outside a particular territory but is also based in several countries and is comprised of members of different nationalities, e.g. Al-Qaeda as an example of an international terrorist organisation.[7]

Civil wars generally adopted numerous domestic terrorist attacks before and during the conflict by the adversaries.[8] These terrorist attacks destroy a nation, economically, socially and politically. These fatalities can easily reduce foreign direct investment[9] which results in lower economic growth.[10] In such a scenario, a poor country cannot fight with the indigenous terrorist group. They may have to seek for foreign support while fighting against such groups.[11] The developing nation's economies are much influenced by such terrorism.[12]

New Classification of Terrorist Group

Local groups of terrorist: Local groups of terrorist which act in well-defined areas, whose action is aimed at addressing the causes of domestic power struggle.

Global terrorist organisations: Global terrorist organisations, which act everywhere in the world to produce major events and attacks that will remain in the collective imagination for a long time. It will be recorded as a historical event in the collective consciousness of the world community for a longer time (for example 9/11 attack on the Twin Towers).

Global terrorist groups: These are groups that act in certain areas of the world with a strategic local action in order to spread global terror, for example German Bakery bomb blast at Pune broadcasted through the internet and media.

Ethno-Nationalist Groups

LTTE—Liberation Tigers of Tamil Eelam (1976) is a Tamil Militant organisation based in northern Sri Lanka. This organisation was founded by Velupillai Prabhakaran to create an independent state of Tamil Ealam in Sri Lanka for Tamil People.

Lehi (Irgun-Israel)—Fighter for the Freedom of Israel was a Zionist paramilitary organisation founded by Avraham Stern 1948. Its aim was to throw out British authorities from Palestine.

PKK (Turkey)—Partiya Karkeren Kurdistane (1978) is an organisation based in Turkey and Iraq, involved in an armed conflict with the Turkish state for achieving an independent Kurdish state.

ETA (Spain)—Euskadi Ta Askatasuna (1959) (Basque and Homeland and Liberty) is an armed leftist Basque nationalist and separatist organisation.

PLO (Palestine)—Palestine Liberation Organisation (1964) was founded by Mahmoud Abbas for the purpose of the liberation of Palestine through armed struggle.

NLG (Algeria) National Liberation Front (1954)—This is a socialist political party in Algeria, and Principle nationalist movement during the Algerian War.

Babbar Khalsa (India)—This is a Sikh militant organisation (1970) organisation for the formation of an independent Sikh state name as Khalistan (Land of the Pure).

MILF (Philippines)—Moro Islamic Liberation Front (1978) is an autonomous region of the Moro people from the central government.

Irredentist Groups

IRA (Northern Ireland) – Provisional Irish Republican Army (United Kingdom, 1969) is a revolutionary organisation from south to end the British rule in Northern Ireland.

JKLF—Jammu Kashmir Liberation Front was founded by Amanullah Khan and Maqbook Bhat in Birmingham, England (1977). It is established in UK, Europe, United States and Middle East. In 1982 it established a branch in Pakistan administered at Azad Kashmir, and in 1987 in Indian administered at Kashmir Valley.

KLA (Kosovo)—Kosovo Liberation Army, an ethnic-Albanian paramilitary organisation, sought the separation of Kosovo from the Federal Republic of Yugoslavia and Serbia in the 1990s.

EOKA (Cyprus)—Ethniki Organosis Kyprion Agonisston (National Organisation of Cypriot Fighters, 1955), was a nationalist organisation with the ultimate goal of "The liberation of Cyprus from the British yoke".

Global terrorist groups have attracted the attention for two very basic reasons: first, the global structure of terrorist organisations is completely new and it adopts a particular morphology that is connected with an analysis called "Skyline Unusual" and, second, it requires a totally new analytical skill because the function of global contemporary terrorism cannot happen without the fundamental contribution of communication and the network of the mass media. From the local groups the global cells have taken the technique of urban warfare and the technique of political attack planned in time and in space. Local claim has strengthened the presence of global terrorist groups. Local terrorist activities are based on local action for global terrorism. This is the hologram of Al Qaeda that appears even when it is not involved covering the international terrorist network that is structured to oppose the global and democratic west, through a management of terror generated by the partnership between international cells and local groups.

Aim of Terrorist Acts

The aim of the terrorist attacks at its core is to create terror; most of the time these attacks have a political purpose. The type of target selected will often reflect motivations and ideologies. Mostly terrorist targets are symbols of authority like government offices, national airlines, banks and multinational corporations. Their aim is to produce widespread fear in public to force the authority to fulfil their demands. They influence and attract media to spread their cause worldwide. The recognition for their cause at a national and local level is helps them to find support in public while harassing and embarrassing government security forces so that the government overreacts and appears repressive.

Hologram Effect

Terrorist propaganda seeks to mobilise domestic and international support, manipulating people's suffering and creating a general sense of fear and vulnerability aimed at destabilising society and its institutions. It is calculated that the more terrorist events are reported in the media, the more visibility and exposure they get. Whenever a terrorist attack is broadcasted, it produces a series of media interference waves: the hologram of terrorism. Hologrammatic terrorism aims to complete the action and ingrain the image of its attack into the world. While it is technically not a holographic image in a strict sense, it lives in us and in our imagination as a nightmare, making threats and risks that may not exist or appear as real. Hologram is three-dimensional image formed by the interference of light beams from a laser or other coherent light source. This optical effect is useful to feed the social massive concern and to influence political decisions. The representation of terror is more efficient than its organisation.

Counter Terrorism Models

Brian Michael Jenkins said that, "Preparedness requires improving intelligence, increasing security and developing effective response capabilities". He explained four defensive methods to face terrorism: Intelligence, Security, Effective Response and Community Involvement. Regarding "Intelligence", countries need to improve with the technological revolutions and update their artificial intelligence with improved technology. The structure of the terrorist organisations changed over a period of the time and it is self-motivated, impulsive, varied, fluid, networked and continuously evolving. Our old organisations are not updated to tackle new challenges. The three largest countries and their intelligence agencies, the United State, Russia and UK, are continuously updating their intelligence. From the "Security" point of view, which is second, it does not mean being limited only for physical security but it can be anything, anywhere and anytime. This is somehow giving the metal threat to common people. Terrorist are attacking trains, subways, hospitals, movie theatres, hotels, nightclubs, banks and many other common spaces. It is not easy for a state to protect every corner of the country. The nature of states should be changed to accept such challenges.

The third is "Effective Response" that refers to the practical preparedness of a country after the attacks. Responsive measures include specialised army or police or civilians units to handle hostage situations, emergency medical and technical team, special trained media and a group of responsible decision makers. The civilian training for such incidents is prominent to deal with attacks. The fourth idea is "Community Involvement" which includes increasing awareness in the public with specific efforts to tackle anxiety. Terrorist attacks create havoc and fear in the society and have psychological effects that persist in people's minds long after the attacks.[13]

Table 1.1: Useful Models for Handling Terrorism

The US Model	*Israeli Model*	*Russia Model*	*The UK Model*	*Proposed strategy*
Overt and aggressive action	Covert action	Heavy and ruthless action	Timely follow up	Exploitation and heavy use of Technology
Zero tolerance	Zero tolerance	Zero tolerance	Understated zero tolerance	Zero tolerance
Exploitation of technology	Pin point target strategy	No Discussions	Preventive and preemptive measures	Eliminate leadership and funding
Avoid casualties	Cause irretrievable damage	Eliminating terrorists even at the cost of endangering lives of friendly population	Effective intelligence	Undercover action
Shaping world opinion				Talks with extremist groups and Integrated Action plan

International Instruments

There are some prominent steps, conventions/protocols by international organisations for protection of civilians from the terrorist activities.

- Protocol for the Suppression of Unlawful Acts of Violence at Airports Serving International Civil Aviation, 1988 (Montreal Protocol).
- Convention on the Prevention and Punishment of Crimes against Internationally Protected Persons including Diplomatic Agents, 1973 (Diplomats Convention, Delhi).
- Convention on the Physical Protection of Nuclear Material, 1979 (Nuclear Convention).
- International Convention against the taking of Hostages, 1979 (Hostages Convention).
- Convention for the Suppression of Unlawful Acts against the Safety of Maritime Navigation, 1988 (Rome Convention).
- Protocol for the Suppression of Unlawful Acts against the Safety of Fixed Platforms Located on the Continental Shelf, 1988 (Rome Protocol).
- Convention on the Marking of Plastic Explosives, 1991 (Explosives Convention).
- International Convention on the Suppression of Terrorist Bombings, 1997 (Bombings Convention).
- International Convention for the Suppression of the Financing of Terrorism, 1999 (Financing Convention) and International Convention for the suppression of Acts of Nuclear Terrorism, 2005.
- Commonwealth Schemes: London, Harare.
- SAARC Convention, 1988, 2006 Protocol.
- These Conventions/Protocols contain provisions for extradition.
- The offences contained in the Conventions are included as extradition crimes.
- Where no extradition treaty exists between the requesting and requested state, the Convention provides the legal basis for extradition.
- Where a State does not extradite it is obliged to prosecute – Au Dedere Au Judicare—"extradite or prosecute".

International Initiatives

The international community is actively elaborating international legal instruments to prevent terrorist acts since 1963 through United Nations and the International Atomic Energy Agency (IAEA). There are 19 universal legal instruments which are dealing with the terrorism. The instruments regarding Civil Aviation are *1963 Convention on Offences and Certain Other Acts Committed on Board Aircraft,*[14] *1970 Convention for the Suppression of Unlawful Seizure of Aircraft,*[15] *1971 Convention for the Suppression of Unlawful Acts against the safety of Civil Aviation,*[16] *1988 Protocol for the Suppression of Unlawful Acts of Violence at Airports Serving International Civil Aviation,* supplementary to the *Convention for the Suppression of Unlawful Acts against the Safety of Civil Aviation,*[17] *2010 Convention on the Suppression of Unlawful Acts Relating to International Civil Aviation,*[18] *2010 Protocol Supplementary to the Convention for the Suppression of Unlawful Seizure of Aircraft,*[19] *2014 Protocol to Amend the Convention on Offences and Certain Acts Committed on Board Aircraft.*[20] Such international legal instruments, Instrument regarding the protection of International Staff, Instrument regarding the taking of Hostages, Instrument regarding the Explosive Material, helped people to believe on international system and international organisations. Some legal instruments directly focused on terrorists like instrument regarding Terrorist Bombings, instrument regarding the Financing of Terrorism and instrument regarding Nuclear Terrorism.[21]

The United Nations General Assembly (UNGA) regulated the Global Counter-Terrorism Strategy on 8 September 2006. This strategy came out with some special global instruments to enhance national, regional and international strategies to counter terrorism. There are four pillars: i) Addressing the conditions conducive to the spread of terrorism; ii) Preventing and combating terrorism; iii) Building state's capacity and strengthening the role of United Nations; iv) Ensuring human rights and the rule of law.[22] The UNSC Resolution 1276 (1999)[23] imposed a limited air embargo and assets freeze on the Taliban.[24] It is also known as the Al-Qaida and Taliban Sanctions Committee. The UNSC Resolution 1373 (2001)[25] is a milestone in counterterrorism adopted after 9/11. This was bounding to all the UN members.

On 17 June 2011, the Security Council collectively passed resolution 1988 (2011)[26] and 1989 (2011).[27] These resolutions were adopting the changing and expanding nature of the new terrorism. The list of individuals and entities subject to the measures would be split in two. In 2015, the UNSC passed the resolution 2253 (2015).[28] This was the expansion of the listing criteria to include individuals and entities helping the Islamic State in Iraq and the Levant also known as Da'esh. The Resolution 2368 (2017)[29] was adopted by UNSC with reaffirmed the asset freeze, travel ban and arms embargo affecting all individuals and entities in ISIL and Al-Qaida List.[30]

Still terrorism as a term and as a subject is much debatable in research and academic community. The wave of the new terrorism is continuing with improved methods and technologies, and posing new challenges world over. To face such challenges from terrorism, countries are changing their intelligence and security. International institutions are also putting efforts to tackle new challenges through different laws and treaties. States should develop new and improved technologies to combat terrorist activities, and have a zero-tolerance attitude towards it. Economic funding for terrorist organisations should be stopped at every corner of the world. The new approach suggested "making peace with talks" for which governments or other groups/organisations can make efforts for talking with extremist group.

Hologram effect of terrorist acts and mass consumption of fear through live coverage in today's globalised world, through sophisticated communication technology and media (both formal and social) is the biggest challenge in front of the world. There is a need to envisage a multi-pronged strategy to tackle new terrorism. There is also a need to develop strong and resilient state institutions and society.

NOTES

1 Ganor, Boaz (2010), "*Defining Terrorism – Is One Man's Terrorist Another Man's Freedom Fighters*", URL: https://www.ict.org.il/Article/1123/Defining-Terrorism-Is-One-Mans-Terrorist-Another-Mans-Freedom-Fighter#gsc.tab=0

2 Hoffman, B. (2006) *Inside Terrorism*, rev. edn., Columbia University Press, New York. See also, Enders, W. and Sandler, T. (2012) *The Political Economy of Terrorism*, 2nd edn., Cambridge University Press, New York.

3 Schmidt, Alex P. & Albert J. Jongman, *Political Terrorism,* New York: Routledge.

4 Crenshaw, M. (2007), "Explaining Suicide Terrorism: A Review Essay", *Security Studies,* 16 (1): 133-162.

5 Walter, E. and Todd Sandler (2002), "The Nature of Modern Terrorism", *The Political Quarterly,* 73(1): 7-24.

6 Fulga, G. (2005), "Combating International Terrorism and Cross-Border Organized Crime", *Conflict Studies Research Centre,* 3.

7 Stephane, L. (2005), "Terrorism Old and New: Counterterrorism in Canada", Police Practice and Research, 6(2): 131.

8 Findley, M.G. and Young, J.K. (2012) Terrorism and civil war: a spatial and temporal approach to a conceptual problem, Perspectives on Politics, 10, 285–305.

9 Abadie, A. and Gardeazabal, J. (2008) Terrorism and the world economy, European Economic Review, 52, 1–27. See also Enders, W. and Sandler, T. (1996) Terrorism and foreign direct investment in Spain and Greece, Kyklos, 49, 331–52.

10 Abadie, A. and Gardeazabal, J. (2003) The economic cost of conflict: a case study of the Basque Country, American Economic Review, 93, 113–32. See also Eckstein, Z. and Tsiddon, D. (2004) Macroeconomic consequences of terror: theory and the case of Israel, Journal of Monetary Economics, 51, 971–1002.

11 Azam, J.-P. and Thelen, V. (2010) Foreign aid versus military intervention in the war on terror, Journal of Conflict Resolution, 54, 237–61. See also Fleck, R.K. and Kilby, C. (2010) Changing aid regimes? US foreign aid from the Cold War to the war on terror, Journal of Development Economics, 91, 185–97.

12 Keefer, P. and Loayza, N. (eds) (2008) Terrorism, Economic Development, and Political Openness, Cambridge University Press, New York.

13 Brian Michael Jenkins, 2004, *The Four Defensive Measures Against Terrorism*, URL: https://www.rand.org/blog/2004/09/the-four-defensive-measures-against-terrorism.html

14 Find the original Document, URL: https://treaties.un.org/doc/db/Terrorism/Conv1-english.pdf

15 Find the original Document, URL: https://treaties.un.org/doc/db/Terrorism/Conv2-english.pdf

16 Find the original Document, URL: https://treaties.un.org/doc/db/Terrorism/Conv3-english.pdf

17 Find the original Document, URL: https://treaties.un.org/doc/db/Terrorism/Conv7-english.pdf

18 Find the original Document https://www.icao.int/secretariat/legal/Administrative%20 Packages/Beijing_Convention_EN.pdf

19 Find the original Document https://www.icao.int/secretariat/legal/Administrative%20 Packages/Beijing_protocol_EN.pdf

20 Find the original Document https://www.icao.int/secretariat/legal/list%20of%20parties/ montreal_prot_2014_en.pdf

21 Find the original Document by the United Nations, URL: http://www.un.org/en/ counterterrorism/legal-instruments.shtml

22 Find the original Document by the United Nations, URL: https://www.un.org/ counterterrorism/ctitf/en/un-global-counter-terrorism-strategy

23 Find the original Document by the United Nations, URL: http://www.un.org/ga/search/ view_doc.asp?symbol=S/RES/1267(1999)

24 Please find the original Document by the United Nations, URL: https://www.un.org/ sc/suborg/en/sanctions/1267

25 Find the original Document by the United Nations, URL: https://www.un.org/sc/ctc/ resources/databases/recommended-international-practices-codes-and-standards/united-nations-security-council-resolution-1373-2001/

26 Find the original Document by the United Nations, URL: http://www.un.org/ga/search/view_doc.asp?symbol=S/RES/1988%20(2011)

27 Find the original Document by the United Nations, URL: http://www.un.org/ga/search/view_doc.asp?symbol=S/RES/1989%20(2011)

28 Find the original Document by the United Nations, URL: http://www.un.org/en/ga/search/view_doc.asp?symbol=S/RES/2253(2015)

29 Find the original Document by the United Nations, URL: http://www.un.org/en/ga/search/view_doc.asp?symbol=S/RES/xxxx(2017)

30 https://www.un.org/sc/suborg/en/sanctions/1267

2

Cheap Surrender and Costly Victory: The Victory Trap

Scott Sigmund Gartner

For the US forces in both Iraq and Afghanistan, quick and decisive conquest gave way rapidly to costly and irresolute occupation. There are many reasons for these seemingly conflicting outcomes. On one hand, the initial victory seemed to result from America's decisive advantages in technology and training, the effective use of airpower, and bad strategic decisions made by the Saddam Hussein and Taliban regimes. On the other hand, the Coalition's descent into a quagmire and long and costly occupation resulted from the lack of US planning, failure to understand cultural and religious schisms, lack of military intelligence, insufficient forces, and bad decision making from the Bush administration. I agree that all of these factors have merit, but here I am interested in larger questions: How does a win turn into a loss, does this inversion represent a larger historical-dynamic? As I show, Iraq and Afghanistan reflect a critical, but frequently unappreciated, pattern between state institutional capacity, war outcomes, and the costs of post-war occupation.

The relationship between war and victory is complex and hard to determine—especially while fighting a conflict.[1] The key to understanding how victory leads to defeat is to recognize two distinct dynamics and the relationship that connects them.

First, scholars have shown that military actions are more likely to occur when conquest is easy and low cost.[2] Second, research shows clearly that the costs of a conflict greatly influence public and political support.[3] The common factor linking the dynamics of conquest and conflict initiation with occupation and casualty sensitivity, and the focus of this analysis, is the status of target state institutions—their institutional capacity and legitimacy—and their implications for both overestimating the ease of victory and underestimating its costs. In short, in the US-Iraq War of 2003, the weakness of Iraq's political institutions (ironically greatly brought on by the US/Coalition 1991 victory) facilitated America's rapid and low-cost conquest of Iraq and simultaneously contributed to the stalemated insurgency, increasingly costly occupation and America's failure to achieve its war aims.

Outcomes like the Iraq War fit into a larger, and frequently ignored, pattern that links victory and post-war occupation. Paying high costs to defeat an adversary is likely to result in specific post-victory conditions, while easy victory can lead to an unexpected violent and costly occupation. Examining the factors contributing to victory in war and success in occupation reveals these conflicting patterns. It further helps to identify the conditions under which states (and especially democracies, which are particularly sensitive to war costs) become involved in the "Victory Trap." A Victory Trap occurs when leaders believe correctly that imposing initial defeat upon an adversary is easy and involves minimal cost, only to be faced with their incorrect estimations of the length and costs of occupation. In the Victory Trap states are lured in by the prospect of easy victory and low costs, and then following what I call "Cheap Surrender," are trapped in seemingly endless and expensive post-war situations.

Both scholars and practitioners often recognize that winning a battle is not the same as winning a war.[4] "Winning the day of battle is not enough.... You have to win the campaign, then the year, then the decade. Victory must usher in political permanence."[5] What they largely fail to recognize, however, are the theoretical links between initial victory and eventual defeat or stalemate.

To understand the linkage between the factors that lure and then trap states, we need to explore: 1) the institutional differences between weak and strong states, the phenomena of failed states and their implications; 2) leaders' preference for low cost victory; 3) the factors that lead to wartime outcomes; 4) the challenge of strategic assessment in war; 5) the critical importance of understanding the factors that systematically influence over and under-estimation of victory and military cost in war; 6) the contradictory influences of adversarial institutions on initial and long-term victory; and 7) how these factors combine to create the "Victory Trap."

Weak States, Strong States, and Failed States

An important way to classify countries is to identify them as either weak, strong or failed states. There are several indicators that help to identify strong and weak states. Strong states, or stable states, have full control over their territories, successfully provide their citizens with high-quality political goods, and perform well in terms of their GDP and on widely recognized indexes such as governmental transparency and HDI. In short, strong states work. In contrast, weak states, also commonly referred to as fragile states, are typically low-income nations with feeble governmental capacity and legitimacy.[6] Weak states tend to have low or decreasing GDP per capita, high levels of corruption, poorly implemented rule of law, and tensions based on ethnic, religious and other conflicts. As a result, they are unable to deliver political goods to their citizens, and combinations of these negative characteristics make weak states vulnerable to crises of a different nature.[7] In short, weak states do not work.

The instability resulting from weak states is often perceived as a source of threat to the international community's security.[8] The World Bank's Country Policy and Institutional Assessment Index is used as one of the most common measures of state fragility, but other indicators, such as the Political Instability Index (PII) and State Fragility Index (SFI), are used as well.[9] Much of the literature studying weak states focuses on case studies of historically fragile states or states that have recently become weak, analyzing the reasons behind their fragility.[10,11] Some studies draw connections between state fragility and other factors, including the availability of natural resources,[12] the concentration of power in the hands of local warlords,[13] and the rise of non-state actors whose political power outweighs that of states.[14] Typical examples of weak states include Pakistan, Sierra Leone, Russia, several nations across the Greater Middle East, and others.[15]

Failed states represent an extreme version of a weak state. A failed state is defined as a political body in which the government has lost political authority and is unable to fulfil the basic responsibilities of a sovereign state.[16] Characteristics of failed states usually include loss of control over their borders, partial or complete loss of government authority, lack of ability to provide public services, and being unable to perform the role of a full member of the international community.[17] However, similar to the case of weak states, there is no consensus on the definition of a failed state, and characteristics and ways to measure the degree of failure vary case by case and scholar by scholar.[18] Research tends to focus on separate aspects of failed states, such as: terrorist activity,[19] gender violence,[20] and abuse of power[21] in failed states. Other studies examine potential ways of strengthening failed states,[22] specific cases of states generally perceived as failed or failing,[23] and debates over states that may or may not be failing (e.g. Mexico).[24] Case studies usually focus on Somalia,[25] Afghanistan,[26] Sudan, South Sudan, Haiti, Yemen, Syria, Iraq, and other, mostly African and Arab countries. The concept of a failed or failing state has been intensely criticized, including for its misleading nature[27] and tendency to juxtapose "successful" states with the "failed" ones.[28] State failure can be measured by indexes such as the Fragile States Index (FSI) (formerly Failed States Index), the Fragility Index (FI), and the State Fragility Index (SFI).[29]

Rather than getting into the specifics of what does or does not lead to a weak or failed state, I think it is useful to conceptualize a continuum, with failed states at one end followed by weak states, somewhat weak states, somewhat strong states and then strong states (Figure 1). The placement of a particular country in one category versus a neighbouring designation (e.g. "weak" versus "somewhat weak" is not critical). Rather, the key factor is that the institutional strength and state capacity of states on the left (failed) side of the continuum is clearly weaker than those on the right (stronger) side of the scale (left and right refer to positions on Figure 1 and not political orientation). This spectrum of variation in institutional capacity has a profound impact on the likelihood of victory in war and the costs of post-war occupation.

Figure 1: Failed State to Strong State Continuum

Failed State	*Weak State*	*Somewhat Weak State*	*Somewhat Strong State*	*Strong State*

Victory in War

A variety of factors affect victory in war, including resolve, strategy, material advantages, troop quality, the objective pursued, and especially the quality and authority of its political institutions—a state's *institutional capacity*.[30] Institutional capacity represents the effectiveness of a government in extracting and organizing its resources. It represents "the creation of *institutions* that are surrounded with some aura of *legitimacy*."[31] A country like Imperial Japan in 1941 had high institutional capacity, while a state like Iraq in 2003 had low institutional capacity.

Institutional capacity plays a major role in affecting a state's abilities to mobilize and direct forces during a war.[32] Think of Nazi Germany. Despite the clear evidence of defeat facing the Third Reich, the enormous numbers of casualties, the material disadvantage, and duration of combat, German citizens and soldiers in 1945 fought until ordered to stop. In the final days of their failed defence of Berlin, the Germans fielded an army of the very young, very old, and many who were infirm. While clearly not as powerful as Guderian's armoured divisions four years earlier, these citizens—who had to know that the end of their nation was near and that their actions would lead to their death – fought with organization and energy, and exacted costs from the vastly superior invading Soviet Army.[33] In fact, throughout World War II, the German Army was able to mount effective military actions despite frequently being outnumbered and outgunned. The German military's tremendous level of organization reflects its ability to draw on the high level of national institutional capacity. That is because Germany, as a country, 'worked'—they were able to organize effectively to fight the Allies (to the Allies detriment).

States with high levels of institutional capacity effectively extract and organize resources and have the ability to create and direct powerful militaries. On the battlefield, they will be able to ask the seemingly impossible of their armed forces, such as to fight as disciplined and organized units in the face of defeat or to move rapidly and with order in the face of victory. Institutional capacity does not mean centralization. As institutional capacity increases, smaller military units that fall out of the command and control system operate independently and effectively. As a result, states with high institutional capacity are bloody and violent foes. Defeat of a big state with high levels of institutional capacity, like Nazi Germany, likely requires massive effort and a war that will be hard-fought, costly, and long.

In contrast, low institutional capacity states make for much less costly and more easily defeated adversaries. A nation like Iraq or the territories of 19th-century Africa lacked the institutional capacity to extract resources from their people and territory.[34] In addition, they were unable to efficiently convert the resources they could extract into powerful and disciplined militaries. In these states, organizations do nothing without orders to act, and institutions are only as competent as their current leaders. On the battlefield, low capacity militaries lack the organization to fight in the face of defeat or the discipline to exploit victories. When cut off from command and control systems, their military forces become useless. For example, Iraqi military units in the Gulf War surrendered in mass even when they held tactical and material advantages, and it was not for lack of courage, as some of these units were veterans of the brutal Iran/Iraq War with demonstratively impressive and tough performance. Even if they are relatively large and seemingly well-equipped, low institutional capacity states tend to have comparatively inept militaries. For major powers, defeating a state with low levels of institutional capacity, like Iraq in 2003, requires a war that is short and low cost.

Victory in Occupation

Post-war occupation represents a common and critical part of a conflict.[35] Whether it is defined as 'post-war', part of the wartime effort or something in between, occupation of a conquered foe clearly represents an elemental part of the wartime policy process. That is, when a war is started in order to achieve a specific set of aims, it is often the case that these aims can only be realized in a post-war scenario. Scenarios can include the creation of new-friendly states (Vichy France), the annexation of territory (Alsace Lorraine), or total occupation and transformation (Germany and Japan). The post-war scenario often represents the goal that initially motivated the conflict or represents the gains resulting from victory. What influences conflict dynamics in occupation?

For a high institutional capacity nation, defeat means that the state agrees to turn over the mechanism of governance and abide by the terms of the surrender agreement. A strong state agrees to command and organizes its resources in line with the terms of the conflict-terminating settlement. Return again to the example of Nazi Germany. What might have been the result of the Axis defeat for the Allies? Germany had demonstrated incredible resolve, fighting effectively despite decreasing prospects for victory and the certainty of tremendous losses. The Nazi ideology deliberately honoured sacrifice and called for the deaths of those that opposed them and threatened the Fatherland. Fanatical resolve exacerbated by one of the most virulent, despicable and transforming ideologies ever experienced in history may have led to an occupation that rivalled the Second World War in terms of blood and duration. Yet the Allied occupation of Nazi Germany was incredibly peaceful. Why? The same factors that helped the Nazis to mobilize resources and orchestrate warfare in the face of defeat also led their citizens to obey the terms of surrender. Remember, Hitler did not surrender Germany (he was dead)—his successor Admiral Dönitz did. Yet, even though Dönitz lacked the leadership history and personal charisma of the Führer, he commanded the institutional capacity of the state. When the state surrendered, so did its army and its people – the war was over.

Conversely, states with low institutional capacity can make for more *costly* occupations. Consider the US occupation of the Philippines, brought about by the American victory in the Spanish American War. At the turn of the 20th century, the US was one of the most powerful countries in the world. The US victory in 1898 against the Spanish had been quick (six months), decisive, and low cost (385 US combat deaths), despite involving the US in battle in both the Pacific and the Caribbean.[36] The occupation, in contrast, involved years of intense fighting that led to 4,234 US deaths (from both hostile and non-hostile action), thousands more Americans wounded, and tens of thousands of Philippine citizen deaths and considerable and conflictual political debate back in America.[37]

The US initially gained great support from the Philippine people by defeating Spain, their longtime imperial occupier. So why was the occupation of the Philippines so costly? The lack of institutional capacity of Imperial Spain meant that the Spanish surrender and the Treaty of Paris exerted no influence on the complex and fragmented Philippine political landscape. Essentially, following the defeat of Spain, the war had just begun. Disjointed politically and spread out geographically, the US had to defeat each insurgent group individually. The result was a long, costly insurgency where the US technological advantages carried little weight.

Cheap Surrender and Costly Victory

Institutional capacity affects both the likelihood of winning interstate war and the probability of fighting a violent insurgency.[38] Critically, these relationships vary in opposing directions. High institutional capacity adversaries represent disciplined, organized states that fight costly wars, but which, after surrendering, have the potential to become a passive and comparatively peaceful occupied territory. Low institutional capacity states are disorganized, undisciplined and easily beaten. But, after they surrender these states have the potential to become actively insurgent, violent occupied territories. The costs for defeating a high institutional capacity state almost entirely result from the interstate war—few costs are likely to be incurred by the victor in the occupation. The costs for defeating a low capacity state result from the violent intrastate occupation, with the initial military defeat representing a high probability, low cost endeavour. As a result of institutional capacity, therefore, wars that involve occupation carry with them a "you can pay now or pay later" set of costs—that is, costs are incurred either upfront in an interstate war or in the back end during the occupation. The key is anticipating these upfront and backend costs.

Costly victories can lead to low cost occupations. Once defeated states with *high* institutional capacity make for more *easily* occupied adversaries. Defeat of Nazi Germany resulted in what I call a "Costly victory"– it cost a lot (in terms of almost every wartime factor imaginable) but resulted in a meaningful surrender that structured the low-cost occupation.

Victory over a weak state may be initially quite cheap—low cost for the victor in lives and resources, but it buys little. The problem with defeating a weak institutional capacity state is that their defeat results in what I call "Cheap Surrender." Cheap surrenders have little impact on the nature of the resulting occupation. Low institutional capacity states have frail institutions and limited control over their people and resources. For example, after the defeat of the Iraq government, organizations dissolved, and the US-led coalition had to start from scratch in order to organize cleanup, and emergency humanitarian and rebuilding activities. Victory over a strong state is costly but has value. Defeating a high institutional capacity state means the victor can mobilize and direct the defeated state's strong and effective institutions. In contrast to Iraq, immediately after defeating the Nazis, UN Forces were able to draw on German organizations to marshal major activities such as cleaning ruble, implementing healthcare, providing safe drinking water, and distributing heating fuel.

What motivates states to become involved in unanticipated costly occupations?

Military Casualties and Politics

Research has demonstrated that citizen military casualties drive wartime domestic politics.[39] Military losses negatively influence public support[40] and individual opinion[41] for a leader and conflict. Casualties also affect policy positions,[42] voter turnout[43] and elections.[44] Recent research has expanded on these dynamics, demonstrating further the extensive impact of wartime casualties on virtually all aspects of domestic politics.[45] The wide-spread perception of the negative impact of wartime military casualties on support, politics, and leaders, has resulted in a preference for low-casualty wars, especially in democracies. This approach helps to understand when leaders make mistakes about estimating a conflict's likely total costs.

Wartime Mistakes

Recent research has demonstrated that there are systematic forces influencing decision makers' decisions to enter a war and their responses once conflict has begun.[46] When debating about what conflicts to initiate, leaders look for those conflicts that they can win. Historically, however, predicting the outcome of a conflict (before it is over), represents a significant challenge. When leaders underestimate the likelihood of victory (thus overestimating the likelihood of defeat) we are less likely to observe them start a war. Correspondingly, we are more likely to observe those wars where leaders overestimate the likelihood of victory (and underestimate the likelihood of defeat).[47] Combining the literatures on casualties and politics, error and victory and initiation together, the key question then becomes, what factors influence leaders to think that war will result in a low-cost victory?

The Mistaken Lure of Iraq

In the 2003 US–Iraq War, the dynamics of a seemingly low cost, quick victory leading to an unexpectedly costly and long insurgency are now clear.[48] Ignoring the domestic political and potentially personal incentives for initiating the conflict, let's examine US perceptions. In March 2003, using the possibility of Saddam Hussein possessing weapons of mass destruction as a reason for invasion, the US-led Coalition rapidly invaded Iraq. Resolution 1441 adopted by the United Nations Security Council in 2002 had given the Iraqi government a chance to comply unless it wanted to "face serious consequences."[49] Before ordering the start of the war, Bush had given Hussein a 48-hour deadline to leave the country, but the Iraqi leader ignored the ultimatum, and on March 19, 2003 American military forces began the strikes.[50] France, Germany, China, and Russia, however, expressed opposition to the resolution authorizing war.[51]

With ostensibly overwhelming force and advanced technology, Coalition forces successfully and rapidly overthrew the Baath regime of Saddam Hussein. In a famous address, President George W. Bush declared Iraq a "victory" on May 1, 2003, in front of a banner that read "Mission Accomplished."[52] Seemingly putting the exclamation point on the claim, Iraqi leader Hussein was captured in December 2003, tried and hung.

American military met little resistance, and by April 14, the US had control over all major centres in Iraq.[53] The invasion was fast and relatively low cost, with only about 150 coalition deaths by May 1. It appeared that the US had achieved a quick and decisive victory over Iraq. Already weak Iraqi institutions, however, were greatly underdone by the American directed dissolution of the Iraqi Army and a number of Iraqi bureaucracies and the forced (and later voluntary) elimination of Baath department heads and leaders.[54] When a series of increasingly violent insurgencies arose throughout the country, the American led-Coalition had no effective local administration to address Iraqi grievances nor a local ally to bear the burden of increasing costly urban fighting. The lack of effective local government and police were especially noticeable in the inability to stop the production and placement of increasingly deadly roadside bombs, known as Improvised Explosive Devices (IEDs), which were especially effective in harming the enormous-logistical needs and thus driving-dependent American forces. By November 2004, this number reached 1,000 and was over 3,000 in 2007.[55] After incurring an increasingly higher number of military casualties, in 2008 the US set a plan for the withdrawal of its forces from Iraq. Official figures for US losses place the total number of Americans killed in action at about 4,424.[56] Further, tens of thousands of US troops were wounded. How did a quick, low cost initial victory turn into a drawn-out and costly conflict? How did the US get Iraq so wrong?

Cheap Talk and Costly Victory

Victory in Iraq represents an example of what I call a "Cheap Surrender." A cheap surrender reflects a defeat that has little value. In comparison, the defeat of the Nazis represents a "Costly Victory." A costly victory represents a wartime triumph that purchases state institutional influences that affect the post-war situation. Thus, like cheap talk and costly signals, cheap victory is easily acquired, but of little to no value, while costly victory is expensive, but has lasting worth. States' attraction to easy, cheap surrenders and avoidance of hard, costly victories lead to the "Victory Trap." To understand these concepts better, I next examine the factors that influence victory in war and ease of political occupation.

The Victory Trap

States, especially democracies, prefer to fight low cost wars.[57] As a result, those states looking to limit their costs are likely to be attracted to low institutional capacity adversaries. The initially small military casualties likely required to defeat a weak state make this type of war appear deceptively low cost. A state unwilling to tolerate high casualties does not want to fight high institutional capacity adversaries who can effectively mobilize and deploy their militaries, because they clearly have the ability to impose great costs. Thus, a state not willing to tolerate high casualties may initiate a war against a low institutional capacity adversary. As a result, these seemingly opportunistic states are likely to win their interstate wars with low costs—*as expected.*

Combat with low institutional capacity regimes, however, may result in violent, drawn out and costly intrastate insurgencies—which are frequently *not expected.* Failure to appreciate the possibility of the continuation of fighting after surrender means commitment to a war that is likely to be more costly than anticipated. As a result, states become involved in conflicts they would have avoided if they more accurately estimated the likely costs. Thus, the Victory Trap affects how states should think about wartime strategic assessment.

What makes the Victory Trap so insidious is that states (like the US) choose to fight low institutional capacity adversaries (like Iraq and Colonial Spain) *because* of their expectations of a low casualty war. States involved in these fights recognize before a war starts that their citizenry will not tolerate paying high costs.[58] Low institutional capacity adversaries, however, make weak losers—defeat is less likely to lead to the termination of conflict. Realization, however, may dawn slowly for those caught in the trap. After all, the initial defeat occurred quickly and at low cost—as anticipated. With interstate war victory as an anchor, troops deployed, reputations on the line, and no anticipation of a costly occupation, it becomes difficult for victors to realize that their expectations for low cost success are misplaced and that they need to terminate their occupation. Those states that fight low-capacity regimes are thus likely to become *trapped* in insurgencies, stuck in a war where they experience *high* costs despite choosing an adversary that they anticipated would only involve *low* cost—knowing, even before the first shot was fired, that they did not have support for a costly conflict and yet becoming enmeshed in one.

Faced with certain high costs, or a roll of the dice, states looking to avoid losses, prefer to fight adversaries that have low institutional capacity than high. For example, it was easier to mobilize American political support for the Spanish American War than World War I. Spain was a weak state with low institutional capacity and an overextended empire. Imperial Germany, on the other hand, was a high institutional capacity state fighting with connected lines of communication and logistics. Moreover, this makes a lot of sense Clearly, in

1898, fighting Spain was going to be easier and less costly for the US, than fighting Germany in 1917, and before each war American political leaders and publics easily discerned these differences. Yet, given the resulting strong opposition to the Spanish American War and the US occupation of the Philippines, it seems highly unlikely that American leaders could have mobilized domestic support for the war if they and the American public had fully understood the actual costs involved. Thus, the key is not to fight more costly wars, but rather to recognize the somewhat deceptive nature of some so-called "low cost" conflicts like the Spanish American and Iraq War.

States not recognizing the effect of institutional capacity to wartime victory and insurgency are likely to see a low institutional capacity state as representing an easy and low-cost target. Colonial Spain and modern Iraq represent states with low institutional capacity that were easily defeated at comparatively low cost (less than 400 US casualties in each case). Defeat of these regimes, however, meant little, and each of these conflicts degenerated into costly, long occupations with a tenfold increase in American deaths. Compare Colonial Spain and Iraq to Germany and Japan. The latter states were defeated at considerably higher costs[59] but victory resulted in dramatically less violent and less lethal occupations (virtually no US deaths occurred in their occupation).

Obviously, for a state, the death of 4,000 of its soldiers is vastly preferred to the loss of 400,000. The question is not which conflicts are costlier; rather the key issue surrounds systematic errors in the ability to estimate costs accurately before a conflict, and the effects these systematic errors in pre-war strategic assessment have on conflict involvement. America entered World War II knowing it would be expensive. This estimate was based on the human and material costs likely to defeat the German and Japan states. The US entered the Spanish American War and the War in Iraq with a belief that the costs would be very low. This estimate failed to account for the casualties incurred in their respective occupations.

Will there be More Traps in the Future?

There are likely to be more Victory Traps in the future. States increasingly recognize the domestic political costs of war. Democracies, in particular, seem to try to avoid costly wars, while making conflicts with apparently easily defeated low institutional capacity adversary exerts a strong appeal. Should the world continue to become more democratic, there will be more states that want to make sure that, if they are involved in a war—especially one for lower stakes—that they fight what they (mis)perceive to be a low-cost adversary. At the same time, the number of failed and weak states, such as Somalia and Afghanistan, has been increasing. As a result, there will be more potentially weak institutional capacity adversaries to take on. These failed states represent clear cases of low institutional capacity. They can be easily defeated, but not easily occupied. More failed states are likely to lead to more Victory Traps with their unanticipated costly occupations.

Lessons from the Iraq War

Contrast the US Civil War and the War in Iraq. The American Confederacy was a comparatively powerful state for 1861. It included a Confederate Congress and Cabinet and had Departments of War, Quartermasters (logistics), and Treasury, which were directed by leaders pursuing a cause that was seen as highly legitimate by their electorate.[60] With a culture promoting rugged individualism (and of course slavery), the Confederate Army fought with high effectiveness against a significantly more populous and industrialized adversary.[61] When Commander-in-Chief General Robert E. Lee ordered his Army to surrender, however, the rebels laid down their weapons and went home. The soldiers' response to Lee was not unique. Shortly after Lee's surrender at Appomattox, Confederate General Nathan B. Forrest gave the order to his riders to surrender. "As always, they followed."[62] What is important to recognize is that Forrest and his men were already fighting as guerrillas, inflicting terrific damage on the North through a brutal and vicious unconventional war. However, they too surrendered peacefully following the surrender of Lee, obeying their commander "as always." Across the South, the Confederate Rebels went quietly back to their homes. The defeat of the Confederacy cost the Union almost 400,000 soldiers, while the occupation was virtually cost-free.[63]

In 2003, Iraq was a weak state. Terrorized by a sadistic leader and his small cadre of sycophants, the state lacked institutional resilience and depth. Deep-seated religious (Sunni vs. Shia) and ethnic (Kurds vs. Arabs) divisions delegitimized the ruling regime and its political institutions, like the Army. Institutional capacity was low. When the US defeated the Iraqis, the government dissolved—leaving no one to surrender to American forces. Casualties in the US in the initial attack were ten times smaller than those experienced in the occupation (as of May 2007). The US fundamentally underestimated what it would take to occupy Iraq and transform it into a stable ally, let alone an operational democracy.

The US has experienced this type of problem before, in the Philippines 100 years ago, in Central America between World Wars I and II, and to a lesser extent in Vietnam. In each case, the approach employed to assess the costs and duration of war with these *weak states* was the same as that used to assess conflicts against *powerful adversaries*, like Germany in World War II.

A key lesson from Iraq is to recognize that there are different types of wars: one where costs are paid upfront in interstate combat (World War II) and one where costs are paid down the road from insurgency (the Philippines, Iraq). These different types of war require different methods of strategic assessment.[64] That is, we need to think differently about a war against a weak state like Iraq in 2003 vs. war against a strong state like Germany in 1941. Failure to employ different strategic assessment procedures leads to entanglement in the Victory Trap.

Conclusion

You get what you pay for. States that are easy to defeat are hard to occupy. Costly victories lead to valuable occupations; cheap surrenders buy little. The defeat of Saddam Hussein, for example, was easy and inexpensive and provided few institutional tools for managing the occupation – a condition dramatically worsened by American policy to disband the Iraq Army and police forces. In comparison, Confederate leaders like Generals Lee and Forrest remained free after the Civil War, after World War II, many German administrators continued their wartime roles during the Allied occupation.

Not all wartime surrenders are the same. The US defeats of modern Iraq and Colonial Spain represent fundamentally different outcomes from the victories over Imperial Japan and Nazi Germany. Victory over the Axis required enormous effort, resources, and loss of life, while defeat of Iraq and Spain was comparatively easy and low cost. Ironically, however, the cost to obtain World War II surrenders led to peaceful post-victory conditions, while the cheaper surrenders of Iraq and Spain resulted in costly occupations. While the costs to occupy Iraq and Spain were orders of magnitude below those required to defeat the Axis, they were considerably more than were anticipated prior to the conflicts.

Policy Suggestion. How to avoid the Victory Trap? The first step is to recognize that war outcomes are not the function of initial battles but rather represent connections between military force, institutions, and politics. The second way to avoid the Victory Trap is to recognize that enemy institutions represent both a threat when attacking and after a potential victory—an ally. This puts a premium on understanding these institutions' strength and not taking actions (like the US did in Iraq) that undermine potentially helpful conquered institutions. Finally, it might be helpful to think of outcomes beyond the somewhat idealized values of 'win' and 'lose' and instead to recognize the complexity of post-war conditions.[65]

States should also be clear about the costs of undermining the internal institutional strength of adversaries. Efforts to weaken enemy institutions might make an initial victory more likely, but they may also dramatically increase the duration and cost of occupation. A more comprehensive perspective on war and its costs should thus require deliberate consideration about the potential long-term costs of trying to create an adversarial failed, or even debilitated, state.

NOTES

1 Gartner, Scott Sigmund. "Wartime Strategic Assessment: Concepts and Challenges", 2015; Blanken, Leo, H Rothstein, and J Lepore (eds.). Assessment of War. Georgetown University Press, 30-45; Sullivan, Patricia. Who wins: Predicting strategic success and failure in armed conflict, Oxford University Press, 2012; Stam, C. Allan. Win, lose, or draw: Domestic politics and the crucible of war. University of Michigan Press, 1999. Gartner, Scott Sigmund. Strategic Assessment in War. New Haven: Yale Univ. Press, 1997.

2 Katagiri, Noriyuki. *Adapting to win: How insurgents fight and defeat foreign states in war.* University of Pennsylvania Press, 2014. Van Evera, Stephen. *Causes of war: Power and the roots of conflict.* Cornell University Press, 2013. Gartner, Scott and Randolph Siverson. War Expansion and War Outcome". *J. of Conflict Resolution*, 40(1), 1996, pp. 4-15.

3 Scott Sigmund Gartner. "The Multiple Effects of Casualties on Public Support for War: An Experimental Approach". *The American Political Science Review*, 2008, 102(1), pp. 95-106; Gartner, Scott Sigmund and Gary M. Segura. "War, Casualties and Public Opinion". *The Journal of Conflict Resolution*, 1998, 42(3), pp. 278-300; Mesquita, Bruce. *The logic of political survival.* MIT Press: Cambridge, MA, 2003; Gartner, Scott Sigmund, et al. "War Casualties, Policy Positions, and the Fate of Legislators". *Political Research Quarterly*, 53(3), 2004, pp. 467–77.

4 Katagiri, Noriyuki. *Adapting to win: How insurgents fight and defeat foreign states in war.* University of Pennsylvania Press, 2014. Sullivan, Patricia. 2012. *Who wins: Predicting strategic success and failure in armed conflict.* Oxford University Press, 2012.

5 Nolan, Cathal J. 2017. *The Allure of Battle*: A history of how wars have been won and lost Oxford: Oxford University Press. Cited in Ian F.W. Beckett, "The Myth of Decisive

Battle." *The Wall Street Journal.* February 25-26, 2017. C5-C6, C5, Accessed October 20, 2018

6 Miner, Steven M., and Ingo Trauschweizer. *Failed states and fragile societies: anew world disorder?* Athens, OH: Ohio University Press, 2014.

7 Miner and Trauschweizer 2014.

8 Patrick, Stewart. *Weak links: fragile states, global threats, and international security.* Oxford New York: Oxford University Press, 2011.

9 Ziaja, Sebastian. "What Do Fragility Indices Measure? Assessing Measurement Procedures and Statistical Proximity." *Zeitschrift Für Vergleichende Politikwissenschaft*, vol. 6, supplement 1, 2012, pp. 39-64.

10 Marques, Margarida M., et. al., "School and Diversity in a Weak State: The Portuguese Case." *Journal of Ethnic & Migration Studies*, vol. 33, issue, 2007, pp. 1145–1168.

11 Walton, Grant W. "Defining Corruption Where the State Is Weak: The Case of Papua New Guinea." *Journal of Development Studies*, vol. 51, issue 1, 2015, pp. 15–31.

12 Bodea, Cristina. "Natural Resources, Weak States and Civil War: Can Rents Stabilize Coup Prone Regimes?" *Policy Research Working Papers*, 2012.

13 Marten, Kimberly Z. *Warlords: Strong-Arm Brokers in Weak States.* Ithaca: Cornell University Press, 2012

14 Saikal, Amin. *Weak States, Strong Societies.* 1st ed. London: I.B. Tauris, 2016.

15 Conteh-Morgan, Earl. "Globalization, State Failure, and Collective Violence: The Case of Sierra Leone." *International Journal of Peace Studies*, vol. 11, no. 2, 2006, pp. 87–104; Kfir, Isaac. "The Crisis of Pakistan: A Dangerously Weak State." *Middle East Review of International Affairs*, vol. 11, no. 3, 2007.

16 Miner and Trauschweizer 2014.

17 "What Does "State Fragility" Mean?" The Fund for Peace: FAQ." The Fund for Peace. http://fundforpeace.org/fsi/frequently-asked-questions/what-does-state-fragility-mean/ Accessed March 18, 2019.

18 Popescu, Alina-Irina, and Valentin Cojanu. "Analysis of Failed States: Some Problems of Definition and Measurement." *Romanian Economic Journal*, vol. 10, no. 25, 2007, pp. 143–162.

19 Piazza, James A. "Incubators of Terror: Do Failed and Failing States Promote Transnational Terrorism?" *International Studies Quarterly*, vol. 52, no. 3, 2008, pp. 469–88.

20 Rodrìguez, Ileana. *Gender Violence in Failed and Democratic States: Besieging Perverse Masculinities.* New York, NY: Palgrave Macmillan, 2016

21 Chomsky, Noam. *Failed States: The Abuse of Power and the Assault on Democracy.* New York: Metropolitan Books/Henry Holt, 2006.

22 Ghani, Ashraf, and Clare Lockhart. *Fixing Failed States: A Framework for Rebuilding a Fractured World.* Oxford New York: Oxford University Press, 2008.

23 Feldmann A. & J. E. Montes, Haiti: Tribunals of a Failed State (Revista de Ciencia Polítіca 28.1, 2006).

24 Derwich, Karol, "Mexico: A Regional Power or a Failed State?" *Polìtica & Sociedade*, vol. 14, no. 30, 2015, pp. 8–26.

25 Menkhaus, Ken. "State Failure, State-Building, and Prospects for A "Functional Failed State" in Somalia. "*The ANNALS of the American Academy of Political and Social Science*, vol. 656, no. 1, 2014, pp. 154–72.

26 Rubin, Barnett R. *The search for peace in Afghanistan: from buffer state to failed state.* New Haven: Yale University Press, 1995.

27 DiJohn, Jonathan. "The Concept, Causes and Consequences of Failed States: A Critical Review of the Literature and Agenda for Research with Specific Reference to Sub-Saharan Africa." *The European Journal of Development Research*, vol. 22, no. 1, 2010, pp. 10–30

28 Wilde, Ralph. "The Skewed Responsibility Narrative of the 'Failed States' Concept." *ILSA Journal of International and Comparative Law*, vol. 9, no. 2, 2003, pp. 425–29.

29 Ferreira, Ines Afonso Roque. "Defining and measuring state fragility: a new proposal." The Annual Bank Conference on Africa, 2015.

30 Maoz, Zeev. "Resolve, Capabilities, and the Outcomes of Interstate Disputes, 1816-1976." *The Journal of Conflict Resolution*, vol. 27, no. 2, 1983, pp. 195-229; Stam, Allan C. *Win, Lose, or Draw.* Ann Arbor: University of Michigan Press, 1996; Reiter, Dan, and Allan Stam. *Democracies at War*. Princeton: Princeton University Press, 2002; Sullivan, Patricia L. "War Aims and War Outcomes: Why Powerful States Lose Limited Wars." *Journal of Conflict Resolution*, vol. 51, issue 3, 2007, pp. 496–524

31 Jackman, Robert W. *Power without Force: The Political Capacity of Nation-States.* Ann Arbor: The University of Michigan Press, 1993, pp. 38, italics in original.

32 Bapat, Navin A. "State Bargaining in Transnational Terrorist Events." *International Studies Quarterly*, vol. 50, issue 1, 2006, pp. 213–229.

33 Weinberg, Gerhard L. *A World at Arms: A Global History of World War II.* NY: Cambridge University Press, 1994

34 Blanken, Leo J. *Rational Empires: Institutional Incentives and Imperial Expansion.* Chicago London: The University of Chicago Press, 2012

35 Lockhart, Sarah (2012). "The Post-War Dilemma: War Outcomes, State Capabilities, and Economic Development after Civil War." Doctoral Thesis, the University of California, Davis.

36 Gartner, Scott Sigmund. "National Defense, Armed Forces, and Veterans." 2006. In, Susan Carter, Scott Sigmund Gartner, Michael Haines, Alan Olmstead, Richard Sutch, and Gavin Wright, Editors in Chief. *Historical Statistics of the United States: Millennial Edition.* NY: Cambridge University Press, pp. 5:333-439

37 Gibney, Frank. "Is President Bush Repeating McKinley's Mistake in the Philippines?" *History News Network*. 28 July 2003. http://historynewsnetwork.org/article/1595. Accessed October 20, 2018.

38 Gartner, Scott Sigmund and Gary M. Segura. *Calculating War: The Public and a Theory of Conflict.* FORTHCOMING. NY: Cambridge University Press.

39 Gartner, Scott Sigmund and Gary M. Segura. "War, Casualties and Public Opinion." *The Journal of Conflict Resolution*, vol. 42, issue 3, 1998, pp. 278-300

40 Gartner, Scott Sigmund. "The Multiple Effects of Casualties on Public Support for War: An Experimental Approach." *The American Political Science Review*, vol. 102, issue 1, 2008, pp. 95-106; Gartner, Scott Sigmund and Gary M. Segura. "Race, Opinion, and Casualties in the Vietnam War." 2000. *The Journal of Politics*, vol.62, issue 1, pp. 115–46; Gartner, Scott Sigmund, Gary M. Segura, and Michael Wilkening. "All Politics Are Local: Local Losses and Individual Attitudes toward the Vietnam War." 1997. *The Journal of Conflict Resolution*, vol. 41, issue 5, pp. 669–94

41 Gartner, Scott Sigmund and Gary M. Segura, and Bethany Barratt. "War Casualties,

Policy Positions, and the Fate of Legislators.". *Political Research Quarterly*, vol. 53, issue 3, 2004, pp. 467–77 (w/G. Segura, B. Barratt).

42 Koch, Michael T., and Stephen P. Nicholson. "Death and Turnout: The Human Costs of War and Voter Participation in Democracies." *American Journal of Political Science*.2015: 1-15

43 Gartner, Scott Sigmund and Gary M. Segura. "All Politics are Still Local: the Iraq War and the 2006 Midterm Elections." *PS: Political Science*. XLI. 2008. (1): 95-100

44 Wells, Matthew. "Casualties, Regime Type and the Outcomes of Wars of Occupation." *Conflict Management and Peace Science* (2015): 1-22; Kriner, Douglas L., and Graham Wilson. "The Elasticity of Reality and British Support for the War in Afghanistan." *The British Journal of Politics and International Relation*.2016: 1-22; Lacina, Bethany. *Public opinion and the costs of civil war–Evidence from the Southern Thailand Insurgency*. Mimeo, 2014; See also: Schwarz, Andreas, Matthew W. Seeger, and Claudia Auer. *The Handbook of International Crisis Communication Research*. New York: John Wiley & Sons, 2016.

45 Reiter and Stam 2002

46 Gartner, Scott Sigmund and Catherine Langlois. "Unbalanced Policy Priorities and the Interrogation of Terror Suspects." 2016. *Foreign Policy Analysis*; Gartner, Scott Sigmund. "All Mistakes Are Not Equal: Intelligence Errors & National Security." 2013.*Intelligence and National Security*, vol.28, issue 5, pp. 634–54

47 Gartner, Scott Sigmund and Randolph Siverson. "War Expansion and War Outcome." 1996. *Journal of Conflict Resolution*, vol. 40, issue 1, pp. 4–15.

48 Thomas Ricks. *Fiasco: The American Military Adventure in Iraq Fiasco: The American Military Adventure in Iraq*. 2006. NY: Penguin Press.

49 Copson, Raymond W. "Iraq War: Background and Issues Overview." *Foreign Affairs, Defense, and Trade Division: CRS Report RL31715 for Congress*, 2003.http://www.au.af.mil/au/awc/awcgate/crs/rl31715.pdf, pp. 1

50 Sanger, David E., and John F. Burns. "Threats and responses: The White House; Bush Orders Start of War on Iraq." *New York Times*. 20 March 2003. Accessed October 20, 2018

51 Henley, Jon, et al. "France, Russia and Germany harden stance." *The Guardian*. 6 March 2003.https://www.theguardian.com/world/2003/mar/06/russia.iraq. Accessed October 20, 2018

52 Sanger, David E. "President Says Military Phase in Iraq has Ended." *The New York Times*. May 2, 2003. Accessed 26 February 2017. http://www.nytimes.com/2003/05/02/international/worldspecial/president-says-military-phase-in-iraq-has-ended.html

53 Copson, Raymond W. "Iraq War: Background and Issues Overview." *Foreign Affairs, Defense, and Trade Division: CRS Report RL31715 for Congress*, 2003.http://www.au.af.mil/au/awc/awcgate/crs/rl31715.pdf

54 Thomas, Ricks E. 2007. *Fiasco: The American Military Adventure in Iraq Fiasco: The American Military Adventure in Iraq, 2003 to 2005*. NY: Penguin Press

55 Gartner Scott Sigmund. "Iraq and Afghanistan through the Lens of US Military Casualties" April 8, 2013. *Small Wars Journal. http://smallwarsjournal.com/jrnl/art/iraq-and-afghanistan-through-the-lens-of-american-military-casualties. Accessed October 20, 2018.*

56 The U.S. Department of Defense. *Operation Iraqi Freedom (OIF) U.S. Casualty Status*. Accessed 24 Feb 2017. https://www.defense.gov/casualty.pdf

57 Reiter and Stam 2002; Siverson. Randolph M. "Democracies and War Participation: In Defense of the Institutional Constrainsts Argument." *European Journal of International Relations*, vol. 1, issue 4, 1995, pp. 481–89.

58 Bueno de Mesquita, Bruce, et al. *The Logic of Political Survival.* Cambridge, MA: MIT Press, 2003; Gartner, Scott Sigmund, et al. "War Casualties, Policy Positions, and the Fate of Legislators." *Political Research Quarterly*, vol. 53, issue 3, 2004, pp. 467–477.

59 Gartner 2006, pp. 5-350.

60 Winik, Jay. *April 1965: The Month that Saved America.* NY: Harper Perennial, 2002

61 Ransom, Roger L. "The Confederate States of America." In, Susan Carter, Scott Sigmund Gartner, Michael Haines, Alan Olmstead, Richard Sutch, and Gavin Wright, Editors in Chief. *Historical Statistics of the United States: Millennial Edition.* NY: Cambridge University Press,2006, pp. 5-773 – 5-80

62 Winik 2002, pp. 321.

63 Gartner 2006.

64 Murray, William S. "A Will to Measure." *Parameters*, vol. XXXI, no. 3, 2001, pp.134–47; Gartner, Scott Sigmund. *Strategic Assessment in War.* New Haven: Yale University Press, 1997

65 Gartner, Scott Sigmund and Leo Blanken. "Beyond Victory and Defeat: Rethinking Outcome, Assessment, and Strategy in Afghanistan." H. Rothstein and J. Arquilla, Editors. 2012. *Afghanistan Endgames.* Washington D.C.: Georgetown University Press, 127–150.

3

Countering Radicalisation and Violent Extremism

Shrinivasrao S. Sohoni I.A.S. (Retd.)

Introduction

This paper examines certain salient features of Radicalisation and Violent Extremism (R&VE), which are burgeoning as incalculably potent threats to national security. Also in the paper, are recommendations towards containing and countering the twin menaces?

Who are the main Instigators of R&VE?

The principal entities prosecuting Radicalisation and Violent Extremism are theocratic Islamist States, chiefly, the Kingdom of Saudi Arabia, Qatar, UAE, and the Islamic Republic of Pakistan.

In tandem with the above-mentioned entities, are other supportive participants endowed with vast financial reserves, mainly oil revenues, and funds derived from the international contraband trade in narcotics and other high-value commodities.

What are their Objectives?

The overarching goal of the aforesaid West Asian entities ostensibly is the subjugation and supplantation, worldwide, of the cultures, belief-systems, values, and the ethos, of entire peoples and countries not subscribing as yet to their beliefs and practices as to the true religion; the real and ultimate goal being global political conquest and domination.

The goal of the Pakistan State, more so its Army leadership, conjoined with Islamist collaborators, is nothing less than to bring about the destruction of India and the conquest of India, and, to that end, to impair and damage India by as many and whichever ways feasible.

What is Happening?

The plain fact thus is that, India is in the focus of a concerted, abundantly resourced multi-dimensional attack, planned by expert practitioners of statecraft and state-destabilisation.

What are the Characteristics of the Challenge?

This threat to our national security, primarily external, has an element of indigenous collaboration, such as from the sectors of organised crime syndicates, violent extremist subversive organisations, and their auxiliary agencies.

Use of ICT and Cyber Space

Stupendous advancement in Information and Communications Technology (ICT) has enabled worldwide non-stop bombardment of target audiences, of data, images, ideas, and impulses.

A new age of international digital warfare has come into being. In this 'New Age War' or New War, factors intrinsic to warfare, such as Geography, Distance, Climate, and Time, have lesser relevance than before.

In New War, Cyber Space being the medium of choice for wielding influence and organising attacks (along with a modicum of local executioners amidst the populace, place, or installation targeted), Old-War requirements such as that of communication lines for physical transport of military assets and ordnance over land, sea, or through air; shore-based support infrastructure; and re-supply resources, are no longer as crucial as they used to be.

There is, therefore, incalculably greater flexibility and ability on the part of entities inimical to India, committed to inflicting profound damage on us, and that too at negligible costs and damage to themselves.

Cyber Space has emerged as the pivotal dimension of waging war in the realm of ideas, ideology, indoctrination, recruitment, mobilisation, and the perpetration of violence.

Involvement of Mercenary Criminal Networks and Certain Religious Institutions

Channels and agencies central to the running of the narcotics trade, organised crime, hawala racket, illicit arms trade, and human trafficking are natural partners in crime for the powers propagating radicalisation and violent extremism.

Certain religious institutions are also important collaborators.

Urban Areas in Focus

There is a sharp focus of efforts to spread radical ideology and violent extremism among India's Youth, congested urban localities (where concealment and clandestine movement is the more difficult to detect), madrassas, mosques, and Sunni Muslim educational institutions.

Youth and Left-leaning Intelligentsia

There is a particular focus on the youth and intelligentsia in liberal arts colleges and other institutions of higher learning, the film industry, journalists, and the artistic and creative community.

Attitude of Mainstream Media (MSM)

MSM generally has been soft on and non-critical of people and parties contributing to radicalisation and violent extremism, and MSM has also been of great assistance (in some cases, knowingly) towards maximising the impact of terrorist acts as desired by terrorist agencies.

For example, live coverage by MSM of terror incidents has not only helped the terrorists, but more crucially their controllers in monitoring and guiding their operation.

Similarly, sympathetic projection of terrorists and their agenda in articles and analytical pieces carried by MSM, and criticism of actions and statements of the authorities, has often come to notice.

Terrorism thrives on coverage in the media. The greater the coverage of terror acts, the greater is the effect produced on the public mind. Without coverage in the media, the psychological effect at by terrorists is minimised.

The main stream media (MSM) including TV and Radio channels, has thus far, by and large, avoided critical analysis of the problem of radicalisation and violent extremism, other than to report violent incidents and occasionally carry some op-ed.

There has been virtually no concerted effort thoroughly to expose the entities involved, and their underlying goals and objectives, plans and programs, and the hypocrisy and criminality intrinsic to their sinister endeavours; nor of the devastation caused to lives of those drawn into radicalisation and violent extremism and the pain, shame, and distress of their families.

The attitude of MSM TV channels appears strongly influenced by political considerations directly related to their alignment with certain political parties, and, in some cases, as well by mercenary considerations (in addition to political considerations) of maximising viewership in countries supporting the activities of terrorists in India.

Political Parties' Position

Certain political parties and politicians have been openly supportive of radical elements and their organisations. The authorities have hitherto, largely, refrained from taking such political parties and politicians to task. Certain political parties and social organisations extend covert support. India's criminal justice system is found wanting in the matter of efficient and appropriate disposal of cases relating to terrorism and violent extremism.

Social Media

Research on social media posts and discourse shows public and personal opinion making and expression thereof has passed through various distinct phases in relation to the problem of radicalisation and violent extremism.

Social media has become a major factor in mass opinion-formation, mass mobilisation, interpersonal communication, encrypted communication, signaling, planning, programming, and monitoring, by terrorist agencies.

Agitations and political campaigns can no longer make headway let alone succeed without skillful and massive use of Social Media.

Constraints on the Authorities

The authorities are seriously handicapped in the matter of preventing misuse of cyberspace by the fact that almost all central servers are located outside India, and the additional fact that India, after its experience in the so-called Emergency of 1975-77, has a zealously guarded tradition of free speech and expression.

Who, Why, and How, do Individuals get Radicalised?

Not poverty, unemployment, or underemployment alone, but a sense of deprivation, insecurity, injustice and overt and covert forms of discrimination, can lead young people, many of whom tend to be educated, to embrace the cult of violence.

Desire for vengeance and morbid mentality, more than any utopian ideal of a so-called just society is what often powerfully drives young people into radicalisation and violent extremism.

The prospect of loot, rapine, opportunity to kill, enslave, and lord over people, has often also proved to be a major attraction; especially when presented as a Qur'anic duty for a believer, and with the additional prospect of assured ascent to Paradise and thus to eternal enjoyment of sensory pleasures promised therein.

Recent studies, particularly in the French newspapers, point out that a few of the people who have taken to ISIS are familiar with the basic principles and goals of their religion, enlist to fight for what they believe is a just, and even a divinely ordained cause.

A sense of solidarity with a wider community of believers worldwide is also afforded.

Most are guided by what they learn about such ideology while surfing the Internet and in chat rooms and other virtual groupings. Trained provocateurs enter the scene and engage individuals for their potential as recruits.

Moreover, many are encouraged to take to violent ways on account of facilitated access to lethal weapons and sophisticated forms of communication, purchasable online and delivered through the same channels that, e.g. reach hawala money or narcotics or other contraband.

Foreign government sponsorship of radical elements and terror groups, and funds that non-State groups receive through the drug trade, fake currency, money laundering, ownership of energy resources, extortion, slave trade, etc., are factors that fuel sectarian conflicts and movements for self-determination.

Radicalisation is a convenient tool to polarize a population, and create and cultivate vote banks—especially in a democracy.

The Kashmir Valley and, increasingly, parts of Uttar Pradesh, Bihar, West Bengal, Maharashtra, and Kerala, are cases in point.

The threat of Political Islam, or Islamism and Violent Extremism will not end so long it is backed by the Pakistan State where Jihadi groups are part and parcel of the State and have State resourcing, equipment, and direction, based on colossal funding available from West Asia to Pakistan for this activity against India.

Radicalisation cannot be reversed nor can extremist violence be contained if both are perceived only as a problem of maintaining local law and order and to be handled only by local authorities responsible for law and order.

The question of Countering Radicalisation and Violent Extremism as a threat to India's national security, may be dealt with a mindfulness of the aforesaid perspective.

Countering Radicalisation and Violent Extremism: Some Recommendations

1. The first requirement towards tackling the problem of Islamist Radicalisation and Violent Extremism is that, State as well as Civil Society institutions nationwide should comprehend the fact that a meticulously planned, heavily resourced, closely coordinated effort is underway, chiefly Pakistan-based, with abundant Arab-funding, and some indigenous collaboration. The overarching goal thereof is nothing short of the destruction and subjugation of India.

   Furthermore, it needs to be comprehended widely, that, Islamist Radicalisation and Violent Extremism, which are in themselves serious threats of far-reaching proportions, complicate and intensify all other dire threats to National Security also.

   Realisation on this basis is of vital importance towards mounting a multi-dimensional strategy efficiently to counter Radicalisation and Violent Extremism.

2. A multi-faceted response, involving the Central Government and its agencies and the State Governments and their agencies, as also Civil Society at various levels and in various sectors, is required to counter radicalisation and violent extremism.

   Whilst a particular Ministry of the Central Government, or a specific Department in each of the State Governments may be responsible, as the case may be to Parliament or the State Legislatures, the task of countering radicalisation and violent extremism involves a range of Ministries of the Central Government and Departments of the State Governments, as also authorities at all levels: Union, State, and District.

Thus, there needs to be sensitisation and appreciation developed in all the above-mentioned institutions, Civil, Military, Police, Security, Central Government, State Governments, District administrations, Educational institutions, Media-related agencies, ICT-related, Cultural, and Religious institutions (to name a few). These need to be acquainted expertly and fully of their respective responsibilities in order to carry out their part of the countervailing effort, and to do so in conjunction and in partnership with others as required.

3. Accordingly, it may be useful to examine carefully whether any new mechanisms need to be created, or existing mechanisms suitably adapted, empowered, and activated, to meet requirements of inter-institutional coordination and direction in the context of the problem of radicalisation and violent extremism.

4. In the above respect, it may be worthwhile to examine the institutional experience and institutional innovations in the developed world, particularly, leading States that operate on the Westminster model of governance.

   Laws and executive instructions generated in such countries may also be useful to examine, with a view suitably to enhancing our own governmental and national capacities effectively to tackle the problem.

5. Government of India and the State Governments need to encourage and facilitate on war-footing, the development of cyber-warfare capacity under official aegis, as well as in Civil Society, to combat the Islamist narrative, propaganda, training, and orientation. This is essential as Islamist radicalisation and violent extremism runs increasingly on the basis of propaganda disseminated round the clock via channels of mass communication, particularly cyberspace.

   Financial and technical resource allocation necessary for the purpose would need to be estimated and provided on high priority.

6. A model of cooperation across Governmental and Civil Society must be developed. This should be in terms of cooperative mechanisms and arrangements. Official Authorities (the Magistracy, Police, Security agencies), must gear up to connect creatively with: Religious Authorities (Mullahs, Maulvis, Alims, Mosque authorities, Waqf heads, Legal experts in Muslim Personal Law), Educational institutions (universities/colleges/vocational education institutions/schools/madrassas); Family institutions

(parents/guardians/society-elders, etc), and suitable sections in the Media (Print, TV, Radio, and Social Media).

Such an approach is better-equipped to tackle the problem, for example, of Youth Radicalisation, than simply relying only on the Police, and their customary practices and procedures of investigation, questioning, and decision-making.

This approach was advised to the State Government of Maharashtra, and on adoption and implementation over the past two years or so, has led to noteworthy positive results. It has since been adopted by the State Governments of Andhra Pradesh, Karnataka, and Odisha as well.

Necessary prior training and orientation of the official personnel involved in such work, is essential.

7. The development of an authentic and authoritative ideological counter-narrative is of first importance, to refute and negate the narrative propagated for radicalisation and violent extremism.

   Experts, citing definitive authorities in Islamic scripture, must base such a counter-narrative on comprehensive Islamic study and argumentation couched in language that may easily be absorbed by a range of lay Muslims.

   Darul-Uloom, Deoband, Saharanpur District, Uttar Pradesh, is now the foremost and most prestigious Islamic teaching and research institution in the world (in the sphere of Qur'anic studies and the Sunnah; more so than even Al Azhar University, in Cairo, Egypt.) Darul Uloom and its Faculty, more than Sufi institutions and experts, (or Barelvi institutions and scholars), has the institutional strength, the institutional commitment and drive, and, above all, the meticulousness and rigorousness of approach needed. Darul Uloom has singlehandedly been combating Violent Extremist propaganda, by its own well-researched and efficiently organised counter-propaganda efforts countrywide.

   It is conceivable that Darul Uloom, Deoband, which hitherto had been keeping itself aloof from successive Governments at the Centre, is sufficiently alarmed by the problem of Islamist Radicalisation and Violent Extremism to be ready and willing to work with Government of India towards tackling the problem.

   It may be considered therefore, whether there is scope for cultivating cooperation between Government and its mechanisms on the one hand, and Darul Uloom and its Faculty on the other, on a symbiotic basis.

A side point in regard to Darul Uloom, Deoband, is that, it is learned that Bangladeshi applicants for Indian visas (to pursue Islamic studies in Darul Uloom), on not succeeding in obtaining an Indian visa, then head to Pakistan for Islamic studies there. As Pakistani institutions of Islamic teaching are heavily funded by Saudi entities promoting Jehadism, they are therefore centres of violent extremism; the Bangladeshi candidates naturally return thoroughly radicalised.

It may be useful to examine whether, without compromising on security, it may be in India's interest to allow the entry of Bangladeshi aspirants into India's institutions of Islamic teaching – in contrast to their heading to Pakistani destinations, becoming radicalised and returning to Bangladesh.

8. History shows us that till 1947, there was a vigorous and continuous discourse between Islamic authorities and scholars of Afghanistan and India. (Like India's Sunni Muslims, Afghanistan's Sunni Muslims predominantly follow the same Fiqh, viz. the Hanafi School of Jurisprudence.) Partition brought about a hiatus which is still not materially bridged—to the detriment of both Afghanistan and India. Encouraging a discourse between the Ullema of both countries would be useful; it is felt, as such interaction will lead to mutual sharing of experience and insights, knowledge, and collaborative initiatives with Ullema of both the countries being anxiety-ridden by the upsurge of Radicalisation and Violent Extremism.

9. It is reported that recent invalidation of high denomination currency notes has dealt a severe blow to Hawala racketeering, and to the use of counterfeit currency—and has thus impacted agendas of sponsors of terrorist organisations and individuals for whom the said denomination currency was stock-in-trade.

   Be that as it may, a concerted supplementary effort is necessary to ensure that alternate means of funding and resourcing Islamist terror groups and radicalisation activity is pre-empted and stopped.

10. Criminal organisations and individuals involved in the narcotics trade, human trafficking, gold smuggling, etc., need particularly to be acted against, as these are reportedly also drawn upon for purposes of the Islamist agenda against India.

11. Mindful of the role generally played thus far by India's 'Mainstream Media', it appears necessary to ponder what may be possible to be done

to alter attitudes of owner-proprietors thereof for the better. The feasibility of very high-level intervention with the said owner-proprietors and their effectiveness may be examined. It would be a most noteworthy achievement if such persons can be convinced that whatever be their political preference in domestic politics, Islamist Radicalisation and Violent Extremism shall impact them also if allowed to go on unchecked, and that the impact can affect their economic prospects as much as their physical well-being; and therefore they need to revise suitably the editorial line and reportage in their information channels—whether Print or Electronic.

12. Of great importance also is to keep up efforts to get MSM to adhere to a Code of Conduct in relation to coverage of terrorist incidents, in particular terrorist incidents when live and underway.

13. It may be useful in this connexion to contrive a test case ending in conviction and severe judicial sentencing of a delinquent news agency – so as to underline the need to observe appropriate media-discipline in the wider public and national interest.

14. It is important in this connexion, for the Government of India to review its news-management policy, especially in regard to panel discussions and talk shows which are watched widely each day.

    The fact is that, currently, the Government of India's position on key issues and incidents germane to Islamic Terrorism, and National Security, are not coming through Government's Official Spokespersons. Panel discussions taking place on TV channels are thus seen as debates between representatives of political parties. Non-official representatives of the ruling coalition are not in a position to state anything authoritatively and convincingly as being the basis on official knowledge and on behalf of the Government of India. In effect, the Government of India thus remains unrepresented. Nor is there a properly publicised press briefing on a daily basis by the Government's Press Information Officer (PIO). The Ministry of External Affairs handles media projection in a much better manner, because of its spokesman regularly briefs the press.

    Public perception is key in countering Radicalisation and Violent Extremism, and the MSM presents news as per its own standpoint – often showing the Government in very poor light.

    It is therefore of the highest importance, for purposes of countering the menace of Radicalisation and Violent Extremism that the Government of India review and restructure its news-management systems and drills so as to ensure that the right outlook is presented in the press for public consumption countrywide in this Information Age.

There is an urgent need to create a panel of 'Government Spokespersons' (as against 'Party Spokespersons') who are articulate and fluent in English, Hindi, and other national languages, and who are trained to appear and debate on the electronic media, with a view to convincing the public at large, on various aspects of official policy, action taken, and other relevant facts that the public at large should know.

The presence of such spokespersons will be of immense value in the Information-War against Radicalisation and Violent Extremism.

15. The US has administrative control over most control-servers. The US has been reluctant, slow, and selective, in the matter of introducing restrictions on internet sites and activity generated by entities involved in prosecuting radicalisation and violent extremism.

    Government of India, in concert with Civil Society both in India and worldwide, should take up with the US Government the question of the need to establish effective curbs, legal and technical, vis-à-vis misuse of cyberspace channels. It may be pressed that, whether the entities involved in sinister misuse of cyberspace appear to target India or any country other than the US, radicalised individuals and organisations with violent extremist agendas do pose a direct threat to the security of the US also.

16. Last but not the least, is the importance of pursuing comprehensive reforms of the police forces of all state governments. These need to embrace not merely the emoluments, housing, and service conditions of police personnel, but training, orientation, and management practices. The system of the 'beat constable' needs to be revived. This will be possible only if there is greater manpower available, i.e. manpower that is also better trained, resourced, and managed. Police reforms are a necessity for National Security, especially towards effectively tackling the alarming dimensions at which the problem of Radicalisation and Violent Extremism is emerging.

Conclusion

The problem of Radicalisation and Violent Extremism has ramifications and an immediacy that cannot, and should not, be underestimated. The actions required for tackling this threat require urgent united approaches between the

State and Civil Society in India, and collaboration with governments and institutions the world over. There are approaches to the problem which if acted upon will save India a great deal of trouble and suffering; and which if not expeditiously undertaken, very serious aggravation and manifestations of the problem will occur.

4

Terrorism and Counterterrorism: Theoretical and Pragmatic Options for India

Dilip Mohite

Terrorism has been as old as human history. It existed during the Greek and Roman times and passed through the history as protest against the state actors, and thereby the state. Theoretically the state has been a normative institution, created with the best of intention of providing highest happiness to the people. It is Plato's idealistic proposition that the state would be able to perform its duty or provide justice, provided its guardians/political actors are moral, ethical and selfless. Though this was considered as the best and desirable character attached to the state but it was never realised. This idea of 'utopia' remained an illusion for mankind. Despite such moral and ethical overtones, the state earned a dubious reputation as a moral and ethical entity, as well as an evil and exploitative one. That is why, thinkers and philosophers indulged in a discourse, which aimed at the creation of the best state, a state with Rousseau's concept of general will or the state which would give in Kantian terms, 'perpetual peace.' Hegel compared the illusory description of the state as 'March of God on the Earth.'

On the other hand, interpretations by Karl Marx, Lenin, Mao, and Trotosky have maligned states as the bourgeois institutions, created to serve the interest of few at the cost of many. It was described as an 'exploitative institution' whose structure remained oppressive, a machine in the hands of few capitalist, wanting to control and possess resources. It is here that one finds clues to the cause of human conflict, based on unjust distribution of resources, and division of mankind into religious ethos, or ethnicity or ideological fraction. John Roll's equitable justice is a case in point. It is this fact that led Marx to say that a revolution will destroy the bourgeois state and create an institution of 'equal people.' Karl Marx's thesis is subject to scrutiny because the socialist society that he claims to be equal and will solve all problems is far from reality. Human greed, power as means for personal gains or claim for just or equitable resources makes mankind divided on several grounds. Niebuhr, categorically states that "none can be perfect, perfect justice being impossible, men become concerned with weighing possible palliatives, with striving for those that promise a little more justice or freedom, security or welfare, and seeking to avoid those that may lead to little less". There are conditions, which cannot be changed but (strive) to minimise unwanted effects. He advocates rules for conduct to create 'conscientious citizen or politician.' The greed for 'collective greed' is a part of political order (Niebuhr).

Tracing the cause of conflict, Morgenthau attributes it to 'scarce resources' where power or struggle for power are a means to an end. Struggle for power, one can explain without reference to evil in men, but more as a survival in the complex world. Man may act individually or collectively depending on the situation or adversary that he is facing. Scarce goods (resources) and evil in man transforms into desire 'animus dominandi,' the desire for power. Further, he (Morganthau) states "power appears as an end in itself, where greater emphasis on the first root of political discord would credit power as an instrument necessary for success in competitive struggles." (Morgenthau, 'scientific man') The above narratives make the following points as linkages and to comprehend the cause of conflict, whether it be for territory, ambition, resources or survival. Human nature has multifarious dimensions, but that is not the crux of this paper. The fact that one derives, though in a hazy manner, is the claim for scarce resources, where mankind organises itself under the banner of ethnicity, religion, race, colour or ideology, but the struggle for power aims at controlling and possessing resources of the nation or world at large. Colonialism, imperialism, hegemony, ideology, sovereignty, etc., are operative norms by which the political order shapes itself into orderly or disorderly world. The cause of conflict (resources) becomes a major factor that divides or unites mankind, which further gets polarised into caste, colour, race, religion, ethnicity, etc. Terrorism is one form of polarisation which creates conflict for power to control and possess resources within the state or globally. Erosion of identity through the forces of globalisation is also another potent factor for conflict (see Joseph Nye and Danhaue) The present day 'terrorism,' with advancements in industrial, scientific and communication and globalisation possesses a 'global outlook' and reach.

Target, Goals and Modus-operandi

The following chart describes the targets of terrorists and the goals and the kind of weapons or tactics used by the existing terrorist groups:

1. **Target:** Public places, trains, bus stations, political actors, tourists, embassies and people who are considered as adversaries or other religious groups.
2. **Goals:** Control over resources, political independence, revenge, free prisoners, weaken governments, create public opinion, etc.
   Method and use of weapons: Use latest rifles (like AK47, etc.), rocket launchers, hand bombs, suicide squads, hijacking bus, aircraft, etc.
3. **Attacks:** Public places, trains, suicide squads, assassination, security forces, etc.
4. **Groups:** Religious, ethnic, political ideologies, right or left wing militants, etc.
5. **Infrastructure:** Training camps with connivance of the state or people in remote areas, regular supply of weapons and funds, leadership, motivational methods, etc.

If we summarise the above six goals in the present context, the world has seen hijacking of passenger aircrafts. From 1970 onwards, the hijacking of Pan Am 73, the attack on Rome Fiumicino airport, the hijacking of Indian Airlines 814 in India are some instances where the aforementioned methods were deployed by terrorists. In 1976, Air France flight 139 was hijacked mainly with Israeli passengers on board. In two cases, Arab prisoners were released, while in the case of IC814, three terrorists were exchanged to save the lives of the Indian passengers, largely, in the hijacked plane. The most dangerous episode in the use of aircraft was the attack of the World Trade Centre and other targets in Washington D.C., New York and Pennsylvania. Since then, air travel or train travel has assumed disproportionate danger to the lives of innocent men, women and children.

The most worrisome news is that terrorist groups are desperately trying to acquire 'dirty bomb' or mini-nuclear devices. Graham Allison has cautioned that with latest use of nano-technology, a football-size nuclear device can be developed, broken it into four pieces and dispatched to the target country. He states that thousands of containers with goods from all over the world are shipped to USA's ports. One such container or three four containers can easily carry such parts in an unassembled manner and create havoc. Though this has not happened but the possibility cannot be ruled out.

Take another instance of the attack on Mumbai (26/11). Few suicide terrorists were smuggled into Mumbai, backed by terrorist organisations, and Pakistan Army (Gen. Durani's latest statement in New Delhi) killed more than 200 innocent people. Besides Mumbai attack, Indian public places, trains and defence installations have been regular targets. Though Pakistan (state) has been involved or its ISI or Army, Pakistan itself has been a victim of terrorism, every week, we hear of suicide bombing and the deaths of a large number of people.

Still, under the pretext of Kashmiri independence, the terrorist/insurgents are given a status of freedom fighters. There are regular training camps in Pakistan Occupied Kashmir (POK) while India is circumspect to take any action. This is because of the fear of it leading to a nuclear escalation. Saira Khan and few other scholars have elaborated on 'low intensity conflict' as a direct outcome of nuclear capability possessed by India and Pakistan. India, apart from appeasement of Pakistan seems to be lacking in devising a foreign policy strategy as well as a strategy to deal with the menace of terrorism. In this respect, there are three factors where India is circumspect or wanting in support from two influential powers, USA and China.

The first factor is that of dealing with terrorists as well as the insurgency menace in Kashmir. The first factor has political and military ramifications. The BJP-PDP government in the State of Jammu and Kashmir has completely failed in maintaining law and order. Under normal circumstances, when such a situation prevails, the centre proposes President's rule under the emergency powers given in the constitution. But so far, domestic politics and gain out of it has prevented the Central Government from taking any action. To everybody's knowledge, the law and order situation would continue to deteriorate if the present BJP-PDP government is allowed to continue. The excessive use of 'force' under the instruction from the Central Government will further result into suppression and violation of human rights which would bring either UNO or human rights organisation into picture. Pavlov's action-reaction theory is worthy of mention here.

This will further bring ISIS and other Islamic Organisations into play, which will be dangerous for India. As such traces of ISIS are found in Lucknow, Kanpur, Bhopal, and Kerala and nearby cities of Mumbai. According to Zartman, the world has turned into 'blue and green' from its original mark of 'blue and red' during the cold war. Can India, with its domestic political, social and economic turmoil, escape further escalation of terror and its goal of pacifying Kashmiri people? Politically, this would be one of the effective methods of countering terrorism and insurgency in Kashmir.

The second factor refers to the role of security forces, which includes army, para-military forces and police. So far, Indian forces are sitting on the fence (border) doing their best to check infiltration. Except, so called surgical strike; it is not a reflection on our brave army or security forces whose valour is acknowledged as the best in the world. But what has India achieved? After the surgical strike, if it was to counter terrorists and terror camps in POK, there have been no relief or reduction in terror attacks in Kashmir or other places in India. This shows that the surgical strike was more of a political tool. Not one surgical strike but several are to be done to curb the menace. India has to convince the related superpowers of its intent to curb terrorism through surgical strikes across the border. If Indian concern is that of nuclear escalation, then Pakistan has to fear more. A nuclear war, according to well-known Pakistani scholar, Zia Mian would 'eliminate Pakistan from the map of the world.' Even Pakistan's sympathizer, direct or indirect, would never approve Pakistan using nuclear weapons against India. Today, their worry is that Pakistan's nuclear weapons or blueprint does not fall in the hands of terrorist organisations. Such a concern is well-founded and it is articulated by Graham Allison and in a fictional form by Tom Clancy 'locked on' India has to device a strong domestic, foreign and strategic policy to deal with the terrorist, let loose by Islamic organisations not only in Pakistan but in Middle East or other parts of the world. So far, the entire security apparatus (Army, BSF, CISF, ITBT, Police) have done a wonderful job with so many constraints but their morale would take a hit if the Indian government does not have a well thought-out counter terrorist policy. Ad hocism is unworkable and dangerous for the security of India. Mere rhetoric by top leaders has not produced any pay offs so far as counter-terrorist measures are concerned.

USA-China and Pakistan

It is pertinent to bring in the role of USA, China and other institutions to device India's counter-terrorist strategy. Can India expect full and unequivocal support from the USA? The answer is yes and a big no. If one takes few historical and geo-strategic factors, Pakistan happens to be its prized possession and the only Islamic country, which is serving the geo-strategic interest of USA. During 1971 Bangladesh war, USA had brought tremendous pressure on India for not venturing into West Pakistan and liberate/settle Kashmir issue. Both, USA and the former Soviet Union didn't want to have a nuclear confrontation for the sake of their formal and informal allies. In brief, USA's strategic interest in Pakistan induces it to connive at some critical issue. The best example is that of acquisition of nuclear capability by Pakistan with the Chinese help. (See *Deception* by Andrian Levi and Catherine Scot Clark). Take another example of Hafeez Saeed. The US has declared a prize of 10 million dollars, and yet for obvious reasons he is practically free. It is possible that the Pakistani government is incapable of arresting him? He has, no doubt the backing of Pak Army, ISI and the people. In short, India is unable to impress USA to curb the activities of Hafeez Saeed and other top leaders involved in terrorising India and planting insurgency in Kashmir. This issue needs to be addressed by the policy makers in Delhi.

The other diplomatic draw back that India faces is vis-a-vis. China. China's interest in Pakistan is increasing ever since the 1962 Indo-China War. Pakistan too has moved closer to China by virtue of Cnanakya's principle, "my friends' enemy is my enemy". In short, the Chinese interest is access to the Arabian Sea, China-Pakistan Economic Corridor (CPEC), Middle East, Afghanistan, Central Asia, etc. (Dilip Mohite, and Bill Emmot). Not supporting India on the arrest or action against Hafeez Saeed, is the best example of Chinese connivance of his terrorist activities, and giving cold shoulder to Indian efforts in the UNO. Both USA and China are competing with each other for strategic foothold in Pakistan. India's diplomatic efforts to counter terrorism draws blank so far as USA and China are concerned. However, India has entered into a pact with USA like 'intelligence sharing', purchase of latest weaponry and electronic network, etc., but it is not enough to support (India's) its counter terrorist strategy. The present trend is favourable to Pakistan, as both USA and China need Pakistan for their respective strategic pay offs. How India can, or has India any strategy to counter the advantage that Pakistan has? A joint module by MEA, Home Ministry, Finance and PMO has to thoughtfully address this issue.

Indian Dilemma

Like USA, some European nations like Great Britain, France, Germany, Italy, etc., are being targeted. The enmity and revenge could be traced into neo-colonialism, neo-imperialism or put it differently a 'global linkage' or John Agnew's para-phrasing 'hegemony without empire.' The entire global politics is affected by geo-economics, sphere for influence and controlling resources. So far Islamic mobilisation is dominated by Oil as the main source of energy, a means to economic prosperity. Saddam Hussain's ambition to control the Middle East Oil resulted in his execution and so was the Iran-US conflict. According to one estimate, the gulf-oil will last for another four to five decades. This has disturbed the activists. Mobilisation under the banner of Islam to control oil and other natural resources of the region resulted into a conflict between the West and the rest. Till this day, ISIS activity or presence in Kashmir has been dismal. (Occasional incidents of using ISIS or Pakistani flags have not posed a serious threat to India. However, recent arrest and of some module from Lucknow and Kanpur has raised alarm in the country.) Michael Klare says in his writing and citing in *Nation* (June 11, 2009) that the 'era of cheap oil is over.' China is almost moving towards being the number one consumer of oil, which not only creates competition in consumption but also its price level. The western control over oil production and distribution has far-reaching implications on 'oil economy.' Producer and consumer, linkage keeps masses out of such deal. It is this point which has created a rift where terrorism comes as a handy tool, resulting into asymmetrical conflict, since the conflict between the most powerful and weak. Such a condition is ideally suited for terrorism as a tool to resolve the issue.

In India's case, it is not oil but a territorial dispute, precipitated by poor economic conditions. According to Military Intelligence Source, a family in Kashmir has more than four to five children, a large family to be supported by a sole bread earner. The poor economic condition is exploited by the adversary (ISI), paid Rs.500 to a young boy for pelting stones on the security forces. Reaction from security forces results into clashes, casualties or deaths. This is how operatives mix up terror or insurgent activities. For the government, a rapid economic development in the form of jobs, cost of living and above all creating a model economic zone in Kashmir would transform the Kashmiri psyche. According to Thomas Friedman, economic incentives lower down the conflict level. Can the government of India and the state government (J&K) work in this direction to take it as a tool to combat terrorism and insurgency? It is necessary to develop a multidimensional plan addressing the causal factors. A module should have political, economic, socio-cultural and psychological remedial measures prepared by top experts.

India is at the moment exercising a soft or defensive military posture on the scene of terror (J&K) and the rest of India is largely handled by the state police in coordination with RAW, IB, ATS, etc. In a way, both suffer from tremendous limitations in taking effective action. For example, the Army has been ordered not to cross the Line of Control (LoC) or take stern military action like USA or Israel. Indian limitations are as follows:

1. India and Pakistan, are nuclear powers. Any aggressive move has the possibility of nuclear war. Putting it differently, there is a military balance by virtue of nuclear capability or Pakistan-China axis. This fact creates tremendous and far-reaching economic, political and strategic consequences. Indian government whose decision-making is more rational and realistic is not geared to take an aggressive course. It has adopted a 'cold start' (in collaboration with security forces) of defensive action. It can drain Pakistan as well as terrorist organisations based across the border. India is equipping its security forces with latest weaponry, radar, and vigilance system to limit its activities but is suffering from infrastructure and financial constraints. Without risking nuclear option, India is largely dependent on its military advantage vis-a-vis Pakistan. Indian calculations are that in due course, Pakistan would dry up its resources and the matter could be brought under control.
   The real problem is with the state police who are doing an excellent job despite limitation of weapons or adequate and latest intelligence network. Attack on Indian Parliament, Mumbai attacks (26/11 and Train and other attacks) were not prevented on account of some basic limitations as mentioned above. If India has to effectively deal with the menace or develop counter-terrorist effective measures, then strong action in terms of training of state police, funds and latest equipment, including 'forensics to detect nuclear terrorism,' is needed keeping the future in mind. India has porous boundaries and the desperation on the part of terrorist convicts to acquire the

dirty bomb (Allison's caution) cannot be ruled out. Like what is reported in *New York Times*, Pentagon has formed a 'nuclear forensic team to deal with the future threat. Indo-US collaboration in this respect should begin at a proper time as not be caught napping (see William Dunlop and Harold Smith). This includes, nuclear forensics, access to debris, access to stockpile data, etc. India should enter into bilateral arrangements by which the data collected could be shared and acted upon. As this may sound far fledged to some but it would be better to be prepared in advance for such contingencies than to delve into the arcane world of nuclear weapons and radio chemistry on the fly.

There are two intrinsic factors that are inter-linked in India. The terrorist factor and insurgency that India faces is a dual threat to its security and integration as a whole. In Kashmir, the Pakistani propaganda all over the world focuses on fight for freedom of Kashmir from India. Insurgency is no doubt present in Kashmir, largely supported by the state of Pakistan, its ISI, Army and radical Islamic Organisations. Both Pakistan and India interpreted this aspect differently. India compares insurgency with terrorism, while Pakistan calls it a liberation movement. Pakistan is trying to draw a parallel between the movement in East Pakistan and what is happening in Kashmir. This makes the situation extremely critical for India, especially from a strategic perspective. Hypothetically, if one views the situation, then independence or Kashmir as part of Pakistan would bring both, Pakistan and China on the doorstep of India. The point is that terrorism and insurgency are two sides of the coin, threatening India's strategic and security interest. Does India have any contingency plan to deal with this kind of threat? Is there coordination between the PMO, MEA, Home, and Finance, Defence ministries that can plan a module to check and overcome this threat? Issues, terrorism and insurgency are juxtaposed to the extent that so far no coordinated steps have been taken to deal with the twin dangers. Besides, India has always shown limitations in its intelligence agencies which is adequately proved during 1965, 1999 Kargil, etc. India lacks technical and financial resources, and above all political will and decision-making ability. If enough care is not taken, the problem of terrorism/insurgency could grow and become unmanageable.

So far, experts in the field have unanimously agreed that Pakistan is the root cause of this problem. So, what solution is envisaged? Break up of Pakistan by encouraging Sindh and Baluchi freedom movement? If Pakistan can openly promote and support terrorism and insurgency in Kashmir, India has above options and it should exercise it without any reservation. The two powers, USA and China may not approve but India has to go ahead so as not to repeat a 1971 story. Also, pressurise Pakistan by declaring it as a 'terror state.' If USA, its own ally can consider this option, why should India hesitate? A powerful country like USA is fighting terrorism with some territorial and military advantage. It is far from its borders and has military/financial technical capability to deter and fight terrorism. India has serious limitations in all three aspects mentioned above. Then what alternative does India has?

Direct and Indirect Goals

The major goal of terrorists is to create fear and terror in the minds of the target country. After 9/11 in USA, every bearded person was looked upon as 'terrorist.' In India too after the major attacks on Parliament, Mumbai attack, especially 26/11, a Muslim was looked upon as a possible terrorist. This feeling was further reinforced by several riots or acts against Muslims; some inflammatory speeches by some key figures also precipitated fear and anxiety amongst general public.

However, the government will have to carefully study direct goals of terrorist groups operating in India. Briefly, the direct goal of terrorist activity is to weaken the state as well as the Union Government and to create fear and panic amongst people. The bold attacks in Mumbai (26/11) exposed governments' weaknesses and limitations to control and deter terrorist activities. As stated earlier, with all limitations, the state police and intelligence agencies are doing an exemplary job. Arrest of some men in Gujarat and UP Police is a case in point. Yet, a constructive and pro-active response would further boost their morale.

The other clear-cut goal designed by India's traditional rival Pakistan is to merge Kashmir with Pakistan. To achieve this goal, Pakistan has been desperately trying since 1948, 1965 and Kargil which was another futile attempt in 1999. Being convinced of its inability to achieve its goal over Kashmir, Pakistan has indulged into 'proxy' war with India. The state-sponsored terrorism against India is the safest bet, knowing that India is circumspect by Pakistan's nuclear deterrence. Moreover, USA and China's indirect support, pampering of Pakistan (to serve their own interest) has been an unabated instigating factor to terrorist organisations, and their attack on India. It serves three major objectives of Pakistan's foreign policy. First, to keep the claim on Kashmir alive and (to) create a world public opinion; second, to foment trouble in Kashmir by giving it a form of 'freedom struggle' or 'terrorists' as freedom fighters or a freedom fighters like Mukti Bahini in East Pakistan. As the days pass by, the situation in Kashmir is becoming serious and may cross the threshold of merely terrorist activity. The third objective would be to bleed India, economically, politically and socially. Economically, India is spending huge amount on fighting terrorism. It is a dent on India's economy from all possible angles. Politically, it exposes Indian government's inability (weakness) to ensure citizens of security in daily life. The terrorist acts in Mumbai, Pune, Ahmedabad, Delhi (attack on Parliament), on Air Force and Army camps have created apprehensions in the minds of people, and undoubtedly shaken their faith in the government. So far, the issue of terrorism has not become an election issue.

Fracture of Indian Social Structure

Socially, it will fracture the Indian social structure further, which is based on certain liberal ideals like liberty, equality, fraternity and above all secularism as the foundation of Indian society and politics. The intra-religious or other conflicts based on region, caste or ethnicity would further weaken the Indian social fabric. Moreover, apart from fracturing Indian society, human rights would become a serious issue, weakening not only Kashmir problem but also branding India as a country incapable of religious tolerance. The recent report by the US Congress is an indicator of this fact. Hence, terrorism would not be aimed at its limited goal of autonomy in Kashmir or North East but may consciously or unconsciously break the foundation of Indian social fabric.

In conclusion, a seven-point formula may be considered as possible and effective measures against terrorism. The argument that terrorism should not be viewed from a narrow angle but a strong will to deal with this menace with a comprehensive plan. Political stability will ensure citizens that the state has the capacity to maintain order, welfare and security, thereby proving its legitimacy. To be able to comply with these aspects, a seven-point formula needs to be viewed seriously by the state of India:

1. Government should clearly spell out its priorities against a possible terrorist attack. This can be inferred from the past experiences, like attack on Indian Parliament, Mumbai attack – 26/11, Air Force, Army or Naval installations, and also base camps and convoys of security forces. It is likely that the think tank of the terrorist organisation is highly professional (backed by ISI or Military intelligence, etc.). They are likely to repeat the targets. Their modus operandi would also look for new targets and new methods to attack. From this perspective, there should be an alertness and anticipation to protect citizens, especially where large groups of people assemble for worship, travel or for any other purpose. Strict vigilance with latest electronic tools and well-trained security personnel can act as deterrence and thereby thwart or reduce the possibility of a terrorist attack.
2. Government and responsible security personnel at the highest level should admit their vulnerability. For example, huge mass of people of Mumbai's Churchgate or CST stations is easy targets. Vigilance of highest quality is a necessity. Take, for example, trains, buses, yet trains and railway station and bus terminals are most vulnerable targets. Security needs to be beefed up at these centers, once again with smart, well-trained security personnel with latest electronic gadgets.
3. The terrorist goal is to effect maximum damage with minimum loss. Human bomb, or car bomb or any such device should be on an expected list on all days and nights. This method is comparatively easy and less costly. The intelligence agencies should be trained and geared to detect such operations by the terrorists. There is no doubt that they may also have bases within India. Detection and identification of these bases by proactive method should be a routine exercise.
4. The Indian government has to develop offensive and defensive strategy to check terrorist attacks and activities. The attacks include cross-border attack on security forces, civilians, hotels, restaurants

and places of worship. There should be strict vigilance on use of sea route to enter India, as well as territorial borders with Nepal, Bangladesh and Myanmar. It would be beneficial for India to enter into bilateral treaties with each country to possibly allow Indian security forces or commandos to enter their territory and eliminate a terrorist network operating against India on their soil.

The defensive strategy also includes strict vigilance within India. One senior Military Intelligence officer admitted about ISI having penetrated into defence forces and many civilian areas. Money and faith are most likely temptations/factors to enroll such anti-state moles. Identification of areas and people who can be used for money or faith should be done on the important bases. Special watch with latest electronic devices should be deployed. USA, Israel and few advanced European countries could be involved in sharing and acquiring latest devices to keep watch on these areas and people.

5. The fifth precaution is to neutralise support, direct or indirect given by some states whose strategic or other interests is involved with a view to weaken India strategically. USA has eloquently blamed terrorist organisations operating within Pakistan or Eastern part of Afghanistan. But, its strategic interest in Pakistan and its government limits its role to completely blame Pakistan for that matter. The perpetrator of 9/11 was of Pakistani origin and so was shelter provided by Pakistan to Osama Bin Laden near Rawalpindi. The connivance of Pakistan in this respect delayed action by US marines for a long time. Therefore, India should convince USA to take stern action on *jihadi* outfits operating freely in Pakistan.

   The other country that connives at terrorist outfits and their anti-India activities is China. China has multiple goals in cultivating Pakistan despite the fact that dozens of Uighurs militants caught in Afghanistan were trained in Pakistan. In a telephonic interview to Reuter Afdullah Mansour, a leader of the Islamic Group in Turkey stated that terrorists are trained in mountainous areas of Pakistan with a plan to attack China. China's Xinjiang province has sizeable Muslim population, which is protesting against anti-Islamic policies of China. Still, China for its strategic gain, which it considers larger than the problem of Uighurs in Xinjiang province, ignores this issue.

Pampering Pakistan-China's attitude on the UN over Hafeez Saeed is a pointer. India has to have a clever and effective diplomatic dealing with China on this issue at the global level.

Ashley Tellis states that China would like India to be confined to South Asian region. It is against India emerging as a 'Great Power' and also going closer to USA. Connivance of state-sponsored terrorism by Pakistan comes as a handy instrument for China. India should have an effective diplomatic policy to deal with China, at least on the issue of terrorism.

6. The sixth point refers to threats, real or genuine or false, to misguide security forces. Quite often, there are false alarms from terrorist outfits to misguide the security forces. It is also likely that some mischievous elements may also make false calls. Under the circumstances, there is an alarm or alert sounded and nothing happens. This is a tricky situation but the security agencies should have proper devices or scrutiny methods to respond to genuine alerts and mischievous calls. Frequent alerts create panic or its effect could be taken as routine or lightly. People and even security personnel tend to take these alerts as routine or do not pay enough attention. In such cases, a quiet action or an exercise should be kept on low key. In other words, the security agencies should act under wrap and not make much show. The terrorist also aims at creating fear and nervousness amongst people and security personnel, and false alarm serves their purpose. Covert measures to deal with intruders from outside or those who are already in the country or part of society. This can be done without big fanfare or publicity to earn accolades from the superiors or society. Of course, the involved men should be adequately rewarded for their prompt and good act.
7. Government, Union and State, should anticipate threats twenty-four hours. Threats could be the established ones and some could be new ones. The most dangerous are suicide squads, like one experienced in Mumbai and the attack on Indian Parliament. The other is routine like planting bombs at public places. In a vast country like India with disgruntled minority, religious fanatics unemployment, illiteracy make the task all the more easy. Here,

therefore, the security agencies should keep a track on old methods and speculate new methods and take precautionary measures.

In a final analysis, India faces the issue of terrorism/insurgency, which is directly threatening security, welfare and integrity. If the issue of Kashmir is not effectively tackled, it will have far-reaching implication on India's goal of pre-eminence in South Asia and more than that to emerge as 'great power' at the global level. The issue of terrorism and India's ambition are closely connected with each other. It would also drain India's economy and encourage other separatist elements to launch such movements. As such Indian history is a witness to such tragedy of subjugation and disintegration. Would history repeat itself? Hence, terrorism is not to be viewed as a local, small or trivial issue, but should rather be viewed with a broad and realistic perspective.

5

Terrorism: Counter Challenges and Military Power

Lt Gen (Retd) D B Shekatkar

If we compute the total number of days (between declaration of war which India was forced to fight and the declaration of ceasefire when the war [was] officially terminated) in the history of independent India, till Dec 2016, the total duration would not be more than 143 days! It means our armed forces, especially the army, fought conventional wars for a little less than six months. If we examine the deployment, employment, direct/indirect involvement of Indian Army in internal security, internal conflicts, namely counter-insurgency, counterterrorism, control of communal violence and so on, it comes to almost four decades!

While the constitutionally defined and assigned principal role of Indian Armed Forces rightly is to protect India from external threats and aggression, protect our territorial integrity and security; there exists a provision to employ the armed forces in internal security (IS) duties to meet IS threats under exceptional circumstances and situations. The operative word of constitutional provision is "Government of India may use the armed forces." Since IS is not the primary role of the armed forces, their services be sought only in rare case where other security forces and agencies have FAILED or proved ineffective to address the problem and effectively handle the emerging situation. The qualifying words are "may" and "exceptional circumstances." But thanks to the wisdom and authority of the authorities who interpret and misinterpret the rules as per their wisdom, have replaced the word "may employ" with "will employ" and the words and concepts of "exceptional circumstances" has been replaced (though unofficially, but in practice) with "any circumstance/situation which the authorities feel appropriate." This has resulted in excessive deployment of army in IS duties over the years. Our experience over the years and the reality on ground proved that there is nearly a permanent deployment of Army in managing internal security. Some elements from navy and air force also support the army in internal security. There is an uncontrollable temptation to involve the army at the slightest pretext.

One of the reasons for the frequent call for army's deployment in internal security is the overconfidence among the bureaucrats (who at times wrongly advise and misguide the political masters) that once called for, the army will somehow or the other mange the problem. It is another matter as to what will be the after effects and implications of such an employment to the nation army. There is also a 'studious awareness' that in case things go wrong due to such frequent employment of army in internal security, none of the policy formulators and decision makers will ever be made answerable or accountable.

As per Carl Van Clausewitz the philosophy and object of war is influenced and decided by politics. His strategic thinking resulted in his famous quote: "War is continuation of politics by other means." It is therefore reasonable to assume that there is a close link between politics and war. If researched and analysed carefully some may, to some extent hold good in the context of internal conflicts, which challenge the internal security environment, and use of military power in managing IS environment. Narrow, momentary political interests of few so-called politicians and political parties in their desire and attempt to challenge the authority of established government create an internal security environment, wherein temptations to use military power is difficult to resist. With the changing perspective of warfare and increasing shift towards a symmetrical, unconventional warfare, the military power will increasingly be used within the geographical limits of a nation and within the society as opposed to wars, which were fought on the borders or across the borders and away from society. To avoid collateral damage to civilian population and property there was a conscious attempt to fight war away from the society. But this may not hold good in future to come. The conflicts internally erupted or externally supported, will have to be resolved within the nation and with the involvement of society, and hence there will be restriction on the use of military power/ combat power in internal security.

While discussing IS challenges and military power an important aspect is that of conflicts in various countries of region and its impact on India. India is a major constituent of South Asia, which is a region of in-built conflicts, internal conflicts which are never ending. In India too we have seen new conflict-zones emerging every decade since independence and none of these internal conflicts are anywhere close to an end. Mizoram has been the only exception. South Asia will continue to be a region of substantial political and military turbulence, which will impact India also. The increase in employment of Army in internal conflicts cannot be ruled out in future. There is likely to be a temptation to employ Indian Army to counter Naxalites, on one pretext or the other. Slowly but steadily Army will find itself totally committed to combat Naxalites.

Lt Gen (Retd) VK Nayar, PVSM, SM, in an article "Civil Military Relations", published in USI journal (Oct-Dec 2008) writes, "Indian Armed Forces like any other institution conditioned by their functional imperative to meet the growing threats to the country. They have also been influenced by societal imperatives; that is why they are different from the Pakistan Army; in-spite of common heritage and traditions of British Indian Army. There is an inherent and natural conflict between the two as military institutions which reflect only social values may be incapable of performing their military role effectively, on the other hand military institutions purely shaped and influenced by military imperatives will be difficult to contain within the society. Interaction and balance between the two is the hub of civil military relations." How true it is when it comes to routine and prolonged use of military power in dealing with internal security situations.

During the initial years of my Army Career, I was inducted into Nagaland along with my Battalion in August 1964 with the primary task of combating insurgency. We see no political solution in sight. Can we draw a conclusion that Army did not use its combat power to combat insurgency? Of course it must be acknowledged that while dealing with internal security situations army does not employ its total combat power. We are probably the only army in the world to have enforced on ourselves the concept and operational philosophy of "use of minimum force" while dealing with internal security situation. It has its own advantage and disadvantages too. But in the long run the philosophy has paid us, though at a very high cost—casualties in the form of our own officers and men. Insurgency in NE started from Nagaland and despite prolonged and sustained operations of army and other paramilitary forces it could not be eliminated. Of course it has been contained and has been "managed" to the so-called "manageable and accepted level of violence" (as the politicians and bureaucrats ably advised by self-appointed experts and analysts prefer to callit)! Does it mean that the "new role" of the army (though not stated clearly in writing) amounts to "manage the conflict" or "manage the violence" and keep it at "acceptable level?" Instead of total elimination of insurgency in Nagaland, it spread to Manipur, Mizoram, Tripura, some parts of Arunachal Pradesh and Assam too. Some insurgent groups are now in the process of organising themselves in Meghalaya also. All this has happened due to political motives of the so-called local politicians and political parties, indifferent and ineffective governing mechanism of states which gave a rise and impetus to separatist tendencies, increase in level of violence, resulting in more and more troops, army units, headquarters, para-military forces, raising of control headquarters and so on. It isn't that the Army is incapable of controlling insurgency but with their vested interests, some political parties, lower rank civil government functionaries, contractors, land, jungle, mining mafia, drug and weapon smugglers want the unrest to continue for their narrow political, monetary and other personal gains. Insurgency, in fact, has become a sort of cottage industry in most of the states of NE. The same will hold good for Naxalites also.

For wrong and narrow political policies and monetary gains in Punjab, the law and order situation got out of control resulting in the large-scale deployment of Army under the name of OPERATION BLUESTAR, and thereafter to combat terrorism. Initially from the deployment of two infantry division size forces the army deployment in Punjab increased to combat terrorism. It was the Indian Army and Punjab Police duly supported and assisted by the people of Punjab, which brought the violence down to quite a level, wherein other steps for resolution of conflict could be initiated from the position of strength. The use of military power during the initial stage of terrorism did help in restoration of normalcy in Punjab which has now been ably ensured by the Punjab Police.

In J&K due to ineffective, incapable and unconcerned governing mechanism in State, the terrorism aggravated. The state administration was totally indifferent to the justified needs and aspirations of simple people of Kashmir valley. The unhappiness towards state administration, dissatisfaction, helplessness and frustration of people of Kashmir was exploited by some local anti-national elements, few so called politicians, supported by some elements of state government functionaries. This was further exploited, encouraged, supported and sustained by Pakistan resulting in a situation of "internal revolt".

Not only Pakistan but also some countries from Middle East and even Europe helped the anti-national elements, in creating an adverse situation for the Government of India. Central Government continued to ignore the inputs and warnings given by Army authorities about the dangerous situation developing in Kashmir. When the situation got out of control again the "panic button" was pressed resulting in large-scale deployment of Army in Kashmir to combat the so-called terrorism, cross-border terrorism, proxy war and low-intensity conflict. In actual fact it was an "insurgency" which subsequently got degraded into terrorism. It needs to be considered that in India there is a tendency and temptation to club everything "under law and order problem". Term "insurgency" indicates revolt or rebellion, and hence neither the state government nor central government wants to accept the fact during initial stages. Once the situation goes beyond control, the tendency is to employ army/military power. From the induction of 8 Mountain Divisions in Kashmir and thereafter the force level has increased quite a bit. New Division Headquarters, Corps Headquarters and Rashtriya Rifle Force Headquarters are the indicators. Though these were desirable, their presence in J&K will be desirable due to peculiar threats from across the border. We should not give up to the demands made by few so-called politicians from Kashmir Valley, to reduce force level. It is to the credit of Indian Army, duly supported by Para military forces, state police, and most important of all people of Kashmir to have brought the violence to manageable level. Of course Navy and Air Force also made useful contribution. Despite great provocation, unacceptable losses to our troops, and junior leaders Indian Army once again enforced on itself the principle of "use of minimum force" while combating terrorism in Kashmir Valley. Nowhere in the world one comes across the "operational philosophy of use of minimum force" in dealing with internal security challenges. Indian Army must be given due credit for this. Even in Sri Lanka, during IPKF operations, Indian Army did not use its full combat power against LTTE, to avoid losses to innocent people, and to avoid collateral damage. Just look at the combat power used by Sri Lanka Armed Forces in combating LTTE. Just look at the combat power used by USA in Iraq, USA and NATO force in Afghanistan and now US Army and Pakistan Armed Forces in Western Pakistan to combat terrorism, Taliban and Al Qaida. There is a temptation among some "think tanks" "specialists", "experts", "analysts" who have never handled a single terrorist to suggest (sitting in air conditioned and isolated environment, far, far away from theatre of operation) that Indian Army should adopt the same operational philosophy and use of preponderance of maximum combat power in our fight against terrorists, insurgents, and to crush insurgency and terrorism the same way as has been done by USA in Iraq and Syria as well as Pakistan in Western Pakistan. This will be an utter foolishness and unacceptable in Indian context. Our self-appointed experts deliberately or otherwise fail to comprehend and accept that US and NATO forces are combating the terrorism on foreign soil in foreign countries, where in there is just no fear or concern to loss of innocent lives and collateral damage due to use of military power. Would they use the military power the same way if they had to combat terrorist or terrorism within the geographical limits of their own country? We must accept the fact that Indian Army operates to respond to internal security challenges within India, among our own people, some of who have been misguided, misled, misinformed and mismanaged. Therefore, the Indian Army will continue to be constrained in using full combat power in dealing with internal security challenges. This will continue to be a biggest challenge to Indian Army.

Even the Naxalite problem which is our own creation due to our ineffective, unconcerned and indifferent local governing mechanism, has been fully exploited, used and abused by just few political parties for their narrow and momentary political gains. Instead of being controlled and eliminated, Naxalite movement has now spread over 13 states and 153 districts of India. Again some self-styled experts have described the 'Red Corridor' running from Nepal (Himalayas) to Indian Ocean or from Pashupati to Tirupati. Every state government has been claiming publicly that they have been able to control or "manage" the Naxalite violence, but "Secretly" sounding the Central Government to deploy Army to combat Naxalites. Home Ministers of India, and even the Prime Minister is on record to state on several occasions, and at several forums that the "greatest threat to India's internal security is from Naxalities". The recent incident in West Bengal (La Lgarh) has clearly proved that the Maoist (Naxalite) threat in West Bengalis an indicator of the growing strength of violent left-wing groups and of the unwillingness of the state to confront them. With an estimated strength (committed Cadre) of around 10,000 all over India, it is not beyond the power of the Central and State governments to defeat, disband, and rehabilitate them over the next couple of years. But through sheer callousness and carelessness, we have allowed a minor threat to grow into a "Frankenstein". One of the state governments seems to have worked out the quantum of troops, as to how many battalions, brigades, divisions, armed helicopters, Special Forces, UAVs will be needed to combat Naxalites in that particular state? It is to the credit of Ministry of Home Affairs, probably based on the advice of the Ministry of Defense and Army HQ, that the temptation to deploy Indian Army in Combating Naxalites has been resisted so far, since it will be a most disastrous course of action .It is hoped that Indian Army does not get committed directly or indirectly in combating Naxalites in future, because the problem is the creation of respective state government and only they can resolve it. There will be attempts to gradually involve the army under the pretext of incidental presence, training in Naxalite infested areas, keep a discrete eye, provide advice, and train the state police and paramilitary forces. This is exactly how army was deployed in Punjab in 1990 to combat terrorism. The initial pretext was that of training and gradually army found them totally committed in counter terrorist operations.

When army is deployed too often and for long durations in internal security for "management and control of violence to acceptable level" (which is a new concept adopted by our governing mechanism since last few years) it places very heavy and professionally unrealistic demands on soldiers, junior leaders and commanders specially up to the rank of colonels (commanding officers of the combat units deployed). The army is organised, equipped, trained oriented and motivated to meet classical conventional and external threats. The troops are trained and motivated to "shoot to kill" the external enemy. The combat philosophy is geared up to use maximum combat power to destroy the enemy and also total destruction and suppression of enemy's capabilities and "will" to offer any resistance during conventional war. We have seen the use of such force recently by USA in Iraq, Afghanistan and by Israel in Lebanon and Gaza strip. IS operations which could be termed as "open ended scenario" with no time limits, run a risk of some civilian casualties and losses; collateral damages to civil property. This leads to wrong perceptions about army's high handedness. Such interpretation is totally wrong. This leads to erosion of "goodwill" amongst the local population where the operations are conducted.

Many local political parties, politicians, the so called NGOs (which are mostly funded from abroad, and some anti-national elements like Hurriyat Conference in Kashmir, are always eager to accuse and malign Government of India and Army by carefully manipulated and twisted projection of events. They misinform our young journalists (both print and electronic) by giving wrong inputs. One should never accuse media. Media has responsibility to the society. They will report what is told to them. There are many incidents of false propaganda against central government and army in Kashmir and North East. Even reputed Channels like BBC have been involved in wrong reporting of events in Kashmir. I have indisputable proof to prove the point. A dangerous feeling of "Us" and "They" is deliberately generated by some local political interests. This adversely affects mental framework and tolerance level of our young soldiers and junior leaders. When soldiers and young officers feel cheated and robbed of their clean image due to false allegations; there emerges a shadow of doubt in their mind; amongst themselves, they start questioning (though they do not voice their views and feeling openly through media which is a good practice) the very purpose and justification and also the usefulness of their prolonged deployment in internal security. Only those commanders who have commanded troops in sensitive, areas, under stressful conditions can realise these facts and harsh ground realities. The people who look up to the army for their security and protection from external threats, due to false propaganda, at times feel antagonised. Thus the army finds itself in a catch-22 situation, wherein the efficient, courageous and exemplary performance of its roles and duties are fraught with the risk of damaging reputation as has recently happened in Assam, Manipur and Kashmir.

Yet another challenge of prolonged deployment of army in internal security is how to avoid adverse impact on conventional preparedness. There is always a danger of "shift" in focus and priorities from classical conventional role of meeting external threats to the daily issues of internal security; since it becomes the immediate major concern of political leadership and bureaucracy. This also impacts the armed forces. Many experts may not agree with me, but this is a harsh truth and reality. One of the examples the shift in the focus from the long term threats from China to combat terrorism in J&K. This shift in focus resulted in thinning out forces from Eastern theatre to boost up the strength in J&K. I do not wish to name the formations, which moved from Eastern theatre to Northern Sector. Have we ever given a thought and consideration to the fact that we may be lured in to complacency and forced to shift our focus from Eastern theatre, and this may be part of some long term well thought of grand design, which can have very serious implications to long term security interests, territorial integrity and stability of India. This issue needs a very serious and honest examination and analysis. Why do we ignore China's claim on Arunachal Pradesh? Are the Chines light hearted, who lay claim to Arunachal Pradesh without any seriousness?

Kargil episode is yet another example of the dangerous implications of "Shift in our focus". "When your adversary finds you totally engrossed in "Internal Security", he will fully exploit the opportunity offered by you on plate. This is what exactly happened in Kargil. While the focus of political leadership, governing mechanism, intelligence agencies and even security mechanism was on Siachen Glacier (number of highly publicised visits of powers that be and media coverage is an indicator) and terrorism in Kashmir Valley, every one ignored Kargil sector. No wonder everyone was taken by surprise in Kargil. Despite of brave front put up by everyone to cover our own inadequacies the harsh fact cannot be ignored. It is to the credit of our brave soldiers, young officers, junior leaders and commanders up to the rank of colonel, that we retrieved Kargil from the hands of our adversary. We ignored the basic they are philosophy of governance "the weak have one weapon; the errors of those who think they are Strong". Our adversary was fully aware of our weaknesses and totally exploited these. If we do not "wake up" now and handle the mechanism carefully we may be surprised again and again. Let us remember the statements of the foreign minister of Pakistan during Kargil war to BBC, that there will be 10 more Kargils. Even General Musharraf has repeatedly said while being in power and after giving up power that Kargil will continue to happen. Let us not make out too much of the "Kargil Report" prepared by some of our eminent experts. Kargil report is nothing else but a cover up of our inadequacies and shift in our focus. No wonder the report is more voluminous than Mahabharat and Ramayan. It is the dangerous shift in our focus that prevented us from anticipating and analyzing as to what was going on in the minds of our adversary both internal and external. Despite all the technological advancements in today's world there is no device, technology, UAVs, and even satellites, which can "read, analyze, and anticipate as to what is going on in the minds of our adversaries". It is hoped that the powers that be of today and in future will not repeat the same mistakes again. Kargil will not happen at Kargil, Kargil like situation can take place anywhere else in India. 26/11 at Mumbai is an example.

It is therefore necessary to understand the implications, limitations and consequences of prolonged employment and use of military power to meet Internal Security Challenges. Prolonged deployment can be counter-productive in long term. After certain length of time and even increase in force levels in a conflict area the "Law of Diminishing Return" starts applying. Military operations and prolonged deployment of army is useful and effective only initially and to some extent.

If we sincerely want to avoid prolonged employment/deployment of army in internal security management, all organs of our governing mechanism, political parties and leadership must send a clear message within India and across borders, that:

> Do not believe in the alliance of money and machine guns; because your children will not inherit the money, but they may end up holding machineguns and bombs which will destroy others and also the children holding the guns.

Internal Security threats, insurgencies, terrorism do not disappear suddenly. Unless a long drawn process of elimination of root causes is ensured internal threats have tendency to resurface in one form or the other. There are limitations of use and usefulness of military power to meet the challenges of internal security.

6

The Saga of Insurgency, Low-intensity Conflicts and Terrorism in Southeast Asia: Tracing ASEAN's Riposte on Counterterrorism

Prof. Tridib Chakraborti

'Terrorism' is a politically loaded phrase. In some contexts, what some see as terrorism may be claimed by others to be the acts of 'freedom fighters'. The struggle of the United Nations (UN) General Assembly to agree on a definition of 'terrorism' demonstrates this clearly. Terrorism is a technique distilled by Sun Tzu 2500 years ago: "Kill one to frighten ten thousand". Dissidents and religious sects to weaken and overrun the established authority since the dawn of civilisation have used by governments to discipline their people and this technique of intimidation. Although terrorism has been a predicament of humanity in the annals of recorded history, it is really unfortunate that till today, there has been no clear-cut definition of this concept.[1] It has been often argued that the word terrorism originated after the French Revolution of 1789. It was first used during the "Reign of Terror" between 1793 and 1794. Yet, there has been no clarity on the meaning of terrorism. The US-based Terrorism Research Center clearly pointed out that terrorism "by nature is difficult to define."[2] Even the Scotland-based Center for the Study of Terrorism and Political Violence (CSTPV) underlines the colossal dilemma in coming out with a proper definition of terrorism.[3] Similarly, the Center on Global Counterterrorism Cooperation (CGCC), an independent think-tank founded by members of the UN and the Council for Asian Terrorism Research (CATR), the largest network of terrorism think-tanks in the Asia Pacific, religiously admits the difficulty of coming out with an accurate meaning of terrorism.[4] Besides this, the League of Nations in the late 1930s endeavoured to define terrorism as "all criminal acts directed against a State and intended or calculated to create a state of terror in the minds of particular persons or groups of persons or the general public."[5] Unfortunately, this definition failed to receive wider acceptance because of conflicting national perceptions on the concept of threat of terrorism. The United Nations in 1999, attempted to draft a definition of terrorism but it also failed to achieve global consensus on account of different domestic considerations among member nations, particularly in the developing world. As against such backdrop, in the socio-political configuration of Southeast Asia, the problems of insurgency, low-intensity conflicts, the issue of terrorism and other threats to these countries are not a new phenomena. Their evolution can be traced to ethnic conflicts, poverty and underdevelopment, domination of ruling party on the minority community, religion (mainly the growth of Islamic fundamentalism), historical legacy, opium and drug-related crimes, military repression, maltreatment on ethnic community, power struggle within various communities, etc. These disturbances were mainly invented as a response to the unwillingness of many Southeast Asian governments to recognise the right of minority's self-determination. In Southeast Asian region, insurgencies and low-intensity wars, the terrorist activities and social unrest are often used by ex-freedom fighters, dissidents, guerrillas, political activists of left or right, ethnic and religious groups, Mafia-style criminal gangs, drug trafficking organisations, authoritarian governments or military rulers and regional and extra-regional powers. This political unrest in the form of guerrilla war and violence frequently varies from one country to another in the region and often challenges the internal security and core foundation of statehood that underscored the post-colonial national identities of the Southeast Asian countries.

The outburst of armed uprising in Southeast Asia is not a current history. Malaysia remains the first victim of the problem of insurgency, before British government left that country in 1957. The Federation of Malaya, under the British rule faced this problem in 1948, organised by a section of disgruntled Chinese people. The British policy makers and administrators, before they left the country firmly handled and skillfully suppressed this communist-led insurgency problem. Thus, the seeds of discontent were temporarily restrained and the long-term effect was much more relentless. Over the years, some countries of Southeast Asia, in order to reduce the separatist tendencies evolved locally by many disgruntled groups against authority, forced state leaderships to furnish concessions of autonomy to minimise the centrifugal pull of independence-oriented aspirations. In other words, the presence of these major internal security challenges was analytic of the lack of legitimacy of the nation-state in Southeast Asia. For example, in Mindanao, offers of heightened autonomy have been critical in integrating Muslim insurgents back into the legitimate political process, as was reflected by the Moro National Liberation Front's acceptance of the Davao Consensus in 1996. In Myanmar, the military junta in November 1996 came to an understanding with a handful of the country's rebel groups[6] about assigning greater ethnic control over regional affairs (including, crucially, non-interference in local drug running activities). In Indonesia, one of the most pervasive issues of contemporary ethnic politics relates to the attempt by the state to deal politically and economically with the grievances of Muslims and other islands communities, who perceive themselves as losing out in the distribution of state patronage. These struggles have existed for a long time in Aceh, East Timor and West Papua/Irian, Kalimantan, etc. In Southern Thailand, greater responsive outlook displayed by the Bangkok government to local ethnic, linguistic and religious demands has been an important factor in helping to mitigate (though not entirely eliminate) the Malay Muslim push for independence.[7]

In spite of these scanty political concessions, separatist tendencies continue to pose an enduring problem for internal and regional stability of the Southeast Asian region. For example, the problems in East Timor (currently resolved), Irian Jaya and Aceh, Southern Philippines, in Cambodia (between Khmer Rouge and Tongkingese/Vietnamese), Myanmar, Southern Thailand, Malaysia, etc., result in suspicion, division and tension among neighbouring countries of Southeast Asia. Further, Malaysia cannot remain uninvolved in the Moro issue in the Southern Philippines, given strong ethnic and religious ties. In the same manner, there have been various allegations by Thai and Indonesian officials of complicity in the Southern Thai Muslim (i.e. Pattani United Liberation Organisation) and Aceh rebellions, which have provoked misgiving between these two countries and resulted in sharp conflicts of opinions and interests and thereby created barriers towards the realisation of a regional security community and a united front against the insurgency, low-intensity conflict and terrorism. This emerging motive of various rebel groups clearly displayed the continuing 'weakness' of the post-colonial state structure and autonomy in Southeast Asia, which itself is a product of the arbitrary imposition of colonial borders that failed to take account of the region's enormous ethno–religious diversity.[8]

After the 11 September 2001 (henceforth 9/11) incident in the United States, the internationalisation of the concept of terrorism, low-intensity conflict and transnational crime have become vital and recognised as dynamic discourses of regional politics in Southeast Asia. Following this event, the entire concept of terrorism changed its discourse from old to new, termed as 'new terrorism'.[9] Currently, the idea of terrorism has multi-dimensional hues, varying from one place to another and it is a politically stimulated form of violence used by both non-state actor and state players. The militant attack by ISIS in a mall in January 2016 at Jakarta has once again brought the issue of terrorism in the limelight in the security domain of Southeast Asia. Therefore, the countries of Southeast Asia are time and again facing the threat related to the issue of terrorism in multiple ways and how to tackle this problem in the post-9/11 world would remain a big strategic challenge not only for the sake of regional security, but also for the long-term feasibility of the regional organisation (ASEAN) itself. Given this backdrop, the purpose of this paper is to highlight the major internal security problems faced by the countries of Southeast Asia over the years and especially after the post-9/11 episode. The paper will also discuss the various counterterrorism measures that the ASEAN has initiated so far to tackle this problem for the sake of regional security and cohesion.

Root Causes behind the Embryonic Development of Low-Intensity Conflict and Terrorism in Southeast Asia

Southeast Asia represents one of the most heterogeneous regions in the world. Although it is generally referred to as a region, the principal source for this designation is the geographic proximity of its component states and the fact that collectively, they occupy the territory between China and the Indian subcontinent. The political system of the countries of Southeast Asia is strikingly varied encompassing a gamut as broad as the differing cultures, religion and divergent historical conditionings that have intensely influenced their character. This divergence of culture and religion, along with other reasons often led to insurgency, terrorism and low-intensity conflict in Southeast Asia for many years. The core roots and causes of separatist identity in many parts of Southeast Asia stem from certain factors: insensitivity to local concerns, regional neglect, poverty (economic marginalisation) and ignorance (lack of education or illiteracy), military repression, ethnic domination of one group by another based on religions, political exclusion and concomitant state repression, historical factors caused by Western colonialism and the forcible subjugation of Islam in Southeast Asia, etc. Over the decades through various academic exercises, it is manifested that terrorist threats in Southeast Asia have evolved from a multifaceted blend of indigenous and external origins that date back to the colonial period.[10] From the existing scholarly work, it is clear that there are three basic schools of thought have explaining the growth and dynamics of terrorism in the Southeast Asian region and they are: the globalist, the regionalist and the nationalist perspectives.[11] Among these approaches, the international terrorism or the **globalist** scholars outline the evolution of terrorism in Southeast Asia from the threat emanating from Al-Qaeda[12] and explain that the Al-Qaeda remains the cornerstone of any meaningful analysis of terrorist threats in the region. From the globalist[13] perspective, the "Al-Qaeda-centric paradigm" strongly links terrorism in Southeast Asia with Osama bin Laden who provided global leadership. The Afghan War of the 1980s was the turning point in the formation of Al-Qaeda's global network of terror that included Southeast Asia. The proponent of this school argues that Al-Qaeda's influence in Southeast Asia spread from the Philippines "where its network is long-standing, well-entrenched and extensive."[14] The **regionalist**[15] school believes that the evolution of terrorism in Southeast Asia is part and parcel of the evolution and development of Jemaah Islamiyah (JI). Although the JI had established global links with Al-Qaeda in the 1990s, the regionalist outlook regards it as "home grown" that pre-dated Al-Qaeda and 9/11. This school believes that Southeast Asian rebels founded JI long before Al-Qaeda reached the region. JI emerged in Southeast Asia not because of Al-Qaeda's global plan but in response to regional conditions and local grievances that existed even before Al-Qaeda was formed. It also felt that the terrorist groups in Southeast Asia are indeed homegrown but "have effectively linked up with transnational organisations like Al-Qaeda."[16] Therefore, the regionalist approach related to the origin and growth of terrorism in Southeast Asia remains exclusively JI oriented rather than Al-Qaeda-centric and for that, knowledge of JI origin, ideology and organisational dynamics is important. Finally, the **nationalist** school approach is challenging the Al-Qaeda-centric and JI-oriented paradigms in Southeast Asian terrorism studies. It argues that terrorism in Southeast Asia can best be understood by analyzing the underlying domestic conditions and national state failures that provide the fertile environment for the emergence of terrorism. This school regards terrorism as a symptom of state failure to address the domestic roots of various armed rebellions in the region.[17]

Over the decades, it is clear that the root causes behind the emergence of low-intensity conflict, insurgency and terrorist threats in Southeast Asia have evolved from a comprehensive blend of indigenous and external origins that date back to the colonial era to present socio-political realities. Andrew T.H. Tan has identified a four-class division of terrorism and insurgency to highlight the complexities of terrorist threats in the region. According to him, the **first** division consists of separatist insurgencies that employ terrorism as part of their strategy. These separatist groups are marginalised and regarded as victims of political exclusion. They carry the features of long-running civil conflicts that pose great challenge to the legitimacy of existing regimes in the region. The **second** division relates to armed anti-government political opposition groups, originated to refute various deeply rooted political, economic and social grievances. These groups have "special operation units", which they use to attract political attention. The **third** division refers to radical Islamist groups aiming to establish an Islamic State through the violent overthrow of the existing governments. These groups clearly justify the use of terrorism through violent extremist ideology and are mostly linked to Al-Qaeda and/or part of what is called the Afghan mujahedeen network. **Finally,** the fourth division is largely based in Indonesia. It pertains to overt and legitimate radical organisations that are sympathetic to radical Islamist groups. Though these groups assert their right to participate in the democratic political process, Tan argues that these groups have the potential to use violence because of their ideological and personal associations with groups involved in multiple terrorist activities.[18] Though poverty (economic marginalisation) and ignorance (lack of education or illiteracy), political exclusion and concomitant state repression, historical factors like Western colonialism and the forcible subjugation of Islam in Southeast Asia are identified as the major causes for the growth of terrorism in Southeast Asia, however to put it in a different way, the present author[19] has identified four prime reasons behind the emergence of low-intensity conflict, insurgency and terrorism in Southeast Asian region. According to him, the crux of this problem boils down to four core reasons: insensitivity to local concerns, regional neglect, military repression, ethnic domination of one group by another and the force of Islam.

Prior to the 9/11 episode, the Heads of the Government of Indonesia, Malaysia, Singapore and the Philippines held a series of meetings in August

2001 and discussed in detail how to deal with the growing Islamic extremists in the region. They expressed severe concern about the large number of Malaysian, Indonesian and Filipino Muslim students who have been going to overseas Islamic religious schools where they came under influence of hardline Islamic teachers. In addition, corrupt law enforcement institutions, a weak judicial system and inadequate cooperation among the Southeast Asian countries made it difficult to eliminate the various insurgent groups that operated in the region. Further, many countries of Southeast Asia have never followed the democratic norms and traditions, alike others in the Third world. Establishment of military regime and absence of democratic tradition, as sometimes promoted by external powers, often dissatisfied the grass-roots population. Maintenance of authoritarian rule without socio-economic development sometimes leads to insurgency, low-intensity conflict and terrorism in some countries of Southeast Asia. Unlike Al-Qaeda's collaborative relationship with the Taliban ruling party and the militia in Afghanistan, Southeast Asian governments have been opposed to terrorist groups and their activities for decades, even if they have not always actively suppressed them. Thus, Islamic fundamentalism appeared a great menace for the entire Southeast Asian region. What are its regional implications?

The biggest obstacle to fighting terrorists in Southeast Asia is separating the fans in the stands from the players on the field. Just because an organisation is Islamic and sympathetic to the plight of Afghans, Palestinians and Kashmiris, does not mean its members are international terrorists. There are more than 200 million Muslims in Southeast Asia. Three countries, Malaysia, Indonesia and Brunei are Muslim majority, and in the world's largest Muslim nation, Indonesia, 170 million people adhere to the Islamic faith. An Islamic fundamentalist upsurge in the multi-racial societies, like Malaysia and Indonesia could tear their social fabric, generating political instability and chaos. This could end their dreams of being economic 'Asian Tigers'. In fact, ASEAN as a potential political and economic force could disintegrate, with Buddhist and Christian countries pulling out. Then democracy would be the biggest causality in the region following the process of democratisation, which has been continuously attempted by these countries since the fall of former Soviet Union.

Besides, Islamic fundamentalism, emerging as a political factor in Southeast Asia, has been a source of concern and could invite external intervention (already ingrained in the Philippines where the US involved its operation against the Abu Sayyaf group). Leaders of Malaysia and Indonesia have already started to seriously ponder over the potential for political instability and disintegration. It would be wise for them to rein in these disruptive forces by restoring liberalism and tolerance, which were the hallmarks of their societies. Islamic fundamentalism initially appeared in Kelantan, North Malaysia and Southern Thailand. Today, the Northern States are under the political control of Islamic fundamentalist parties. Its appearance in Indonesia has been only in the recent past and especially after President Suharto's fall. Islamic fundamentalist terrorism has also been quite prominent in the Christian state of the Philippines, where western tourists are being held hostage. Thus, the moot question is why Islamic communities in Southeast Asia, long known for tolerance and liberalism, fell prey to the West Asian brand of Islamic fundamentalism? There is no doubt that Saudi and Gulf States' money has largely accelerated their fundamentalist activities. But regional economic disparities within the states remain an important reason behind their uprising. It is from these economically backward regions that there has been a large outflow of young people to theological seminars in Pakistan and Saudi Arabia in the last 10-15 years. It has flourished because it became a tool in electoral politics in many countries of Southeast Asia. Thus, the above mentioned reasons behind the growth of insurgency, low-intensity conflicts and terrorism clearly reflect the current reality. The countries of Southeast Asia, after the 9/11 incident, cannot avoid the security implications of the worldwide radicalisation and emergence of post-modern terrorism.

The Ascent of Multiple Terrorist Groups in Southeast Asian Turf

As trans-border-/borderless crime, insurgency, low-intensity conflict and terrorism, by nature are international problems that require a solution with an international focus, for a global coalition against terrorism to succeed governments must be held accountable for eliminating their local terrorist threats. Even before the attack of World Trade Centre on 11 September 2001, insurgencies, low-intensity conflicts and terrorism in Southeast Asia had sometimes severely embittered bilateral relations among the ASEAN states because of their trans-boundary character. As against such backdrop, in recent times, the growth of ISIS and its expanding wings all over the globe has changed the entire dynamics of terrorist discourse in the domain of Europe, Southeast Asia and beyond. Although the countries of Southeast Asia had a long-drawn experience of low-intensity conflict and insurgency problem for more than five decades, but the dynamics of the threat gradually shifted following the

9/11 incident. While mapping out terrorist groups in Southeast Asia, the US State Department identified three main groups as listed by Foreign Terrorist Organisations (FTOs): JI (Indonesia), Abu Sayyaf Group (ASG, the Philippines) and the Communist Party of the Philippines/New Peoples' Army (CPP/NPA, the Philippines).[20] Added to this, Al Qaeda also remains a major terrorist organisation, which is actively involved with reference to the issue of terrorism in Southeast Asia. This resulted in that many of these groups threaten the *status quo* of the region by seeking to create independent Islamic states in majority-Muslim areas, overthrow existing secular governments, and/or establish a new supra-national Islamic state encompassing Indonesia, Malaysia, Singapore, the southern Philippines, and southern Thailand. In recent years, with the gradual wane of Al Qaeda network, the ISIS re-surfaced in the turf of Southeast Asian countries and has emerged once again as a major security threat for the region.

While tracing the roots behind the emergence of radical Islamic movements in Southeast Asia from early-to-mid 1990s, mainly the emergence of Al Qaeda terrorist network was most prominent among the following factors. Other factors include reaction to globalisation, which has been particularly associated with the United States in the minds of regional elites; frustration with repression by secularist governments; the desire to create a pan-Islamic Southeast Asia; reaction to the Israeli occupation in the West Bank and Gaza Strip; and the arrival of terrorist veterans of years of fighting in Afghanistan.[21] The Al Qaeda militants in the turf of Southeast Asia, who have been primarily of Middle Eastern origin, appear to have performed three primary tasks. **First,** they set up local cells, predominantly headed by Arab members of Al Qaeda, which provided regional offices supporting the network's global operations. These cells have exploited the region's generally loose border controls to hold meetings in Southeast Asia to plan attacks against Western targets, horde operatives transiting through Southeast Asia, and provide safe haven for other operatives fleeing U.S. intelligence services. In the late 1990s, the focus of Al Qaeda's Southeast Asia activity appears to have moved to Malaysia, Singapore, and Indonesia. Al Qaeda's leadership has also taken advantage of Southeast Asia's generally loose financial controls to use various countries in the region as places to raise, transmit, and launder the network's funds. **Secondly,** over time, Al Qaeda Southeast Asian operatives helped to create what may be Southeast Asia's first indigenous regional terrorist network, Jemaah Islamiyah, which has plotted attacks against Western targets. **Thirdly,** Al Qaeda's local cells worked to assist indigenous radical Islamic groups with money and training.

Until it was broken up in the mid-1990s, Al Qaeda's Manila cell provided extensive financial assistance to Moro militants such as the Abu Sayyaf Group and the Moro Islamic Liberation Front (MILF).[22] Hence, before the 9/11 event, international terrorist incidents in the region of Southeast Asia recorded only a total of 186 international terrorist incidents from 1984–96 compared to 2,073 attacks in Europe, 1,631 attacks in Latin American, 1,392 attacks in the Middle East and 362 attacks in Africa.[23] However, this situation changed route in the post-9/11 world.

The Counterterrorist Initiatives by Southeast Asian Countries before 9/11

The countries of Southeast Asia, before the 9/11 incident, regarded terrorist threats in the region as low-level. Some governments in fact viewed the existence of terrorist cells in their countries on account of existent domestic political environment. As against such backdrop, before the 9/11 incident, the ASEAN members tried to promote their cooperation in combating transnational crimes since 1976, concentrating on narcotics trafficking, but later the crimes have intensified in both degree and forms. They involved terrorism, arms smuggling, illegal money laundering, smuggling of illegal migrants, piracy and organised crime, etc. Hence, in different Conferences and Summit meetings, the ASEAN members had taken resolutions regarding the problem of transnational crimes and insurgencies. Starting in 1996, the ASEAN countries turned their attention to a more diversified list of organised crimes that transcend national boundaries, such as terrorism, arms smuggling, and money laundering, trafficking in women and children, piracy and new types of drug abuse and trafficking.[24]

At the 29th ASEAN Ministerial Meeting held in Jakarta on 20 July 1996, the Ministers agreed on the following: "recognising the need to focus attention on such crimes such as narcotics, economic crimes, including money laundering, environmental and illegal migration which transcend borders and affects the lives of the people in the region. The Meeting agreed to share the view that the management of such transnational issues is urgently called for so that they would not affect the long term viability of ASEAN and its individual member nations."[25] Following this decision, on 20 December 1997, in Manila, the first meeting of ASEAN Expert on Transnational Crime took place. The meeting agreed to adopt the ASEAN Declaration on Transnational Crime and questionably underscored the collective commitment of ASEAN member states to co-operate in their efforts against transnational criminal activity and it nonetheless adhered to the 'ASEAN Way' of decision-making by consensus and the reliance on non-binding rules.[26] In line with the implementation of the ASEAN Declaration on Transnational Crime, an Ad-hoc ASEAN Experts Group Meeting on Transnational Crime was held in Manila, on 24–26 November 1998. This meeting succeeded in formulating the ASEAN Plan of Action to combat Transnational Crime and agreed to recommend a Plan of Action, together with its suggestion to include various ASEAN bodies into the institutional framework in combating transnational crime and forwarded a proposal for the establishment for the ASEAN Centre on Transnational Crime in Manila.[27] However, despite their collective acknowledgement of terrorism as a transnational phenomenon, little concrete progress was made until the game-changing impact of the 9/11 events, which brought the terrorism issue to the forefront of national and regional security agendas.

The 11 September Episode and its Impact on the Economy of Southeast Asia

On 11 September 2001, an apparently well-financed and coordinated attack by terrorists into each of the New York World Trade Centre's Towers brought back a rather neglected discourse of terrorism in the international politics to the forefront. These terrorist strikes in the US were truly a defining moment in the evolution of the attitude of the US and other countries of the West, towards international cooperation with the non-Western countries in dealing with terrorism, domestic or international.[28] Although the issue of terrorism created a severe impact in the social, economic and military sphere on the countries of Southeast Asia over the past four decades, the propensity reached its nadir especially after the 9/11 terrorist incidence. In this region, the impact was relentless, which resulted in financial losses of nearly $80-$90 billion.[29] The after-effect was the vulnerability of the region and financial consequences were particularly heavy in multiple areas, like the airline industry, tourism, and insurance sector, foreign investment, conflict casualties and displaced persons, social impact, increase in defense expenditure, etc. **First**, there was decline in tourism sector. It has been estimated that after the Bali bombing, demands for local hotels dropped to 27 per cent and the Asian Development Bank estimated tourist arrivals in Indonesia had fallen by 38 per cent. To the countries of Southeast Asia, tourism is a critical source of revenue generation and remains a major component of economic development. The political unrest on account of terrorism severely affected the tourist industry, which brings in about US $5 billion a year, and the loss of jobs nearly 150,000.[30] Besides this, terrorism has also affected foreign direct investments (FDI) in Southeast Asia. **Secondly,** fight against terrorism and for those military operations in the region brought huge civilian casualties and led to a large number of internally displaced persons (IDPs). In this region, 600,000 IDPs were recorded in Burma, 750,000 in Indonesia and 500,000 in the Philippines.[31] In fact, the Internal Displacement Monitoring Centre based in Norway in 2008, roughly estimated that there were around 3.5 million IDPs in Southeast Asia, with an increase of 400,000 compared to the end of 2007.[32] These IDPs mostly were victims of counterinsurgency operations and war on terrorism in the region. **Thirdly,** fall in income and lack of basic services, mainly health, education and other state's social welfare services, remains another vital factor which deeply affected the countries of Southeast Asia, in connection with terrorist threats and counterterrorism measures. Terrorist attacks on tourist spots, hotels, transport systems and other multiple areas resulted in the decline of income and a loss of almost 3 per cent growth in the entire region, where major terrorist attacks occurred after 9/11.[33] **Finally,** terrorist threat and counterterrorism efforts in Southeast Asia also created a harsh impact on the military budget of regional states. Immediately after 9/11 episode, defense spending increased noticeably to tackle terrorism threats. In fact, it is estimated that military spending increased nearly to 9 per cent.[34] Many countries in this region engaged in acquisitions of coastal patrol vessels, corvettes, missile boats, and maritime patrol aircraft, initiated to build fighter aircraft, major naval combatant vessels, and worked to enhance their submarine and missile capacities.[35] Another important reason behind the increase of defence budget is that most of the countries of Southeast Asia have strategic sea-lanes. The sea is a major source of food for the region, and the sea-lanes are the lifeline of these countries, since their economies are heavily dependent on unimpeded access to raw materials, market and investment opportunities. All these countries have depended on the free passage of goods across the seas, and the majority with their export-oriented economic structure, have depended even more on maritime transportation. So, safeguarding vital sea lanes and uninterrupted and secure flow of shipping is critical for survival and prosperity of regional countries. Over the years, the multiple terrorist groups have used the sea to transport weapons, move forces, piracy, smuggling, illegal migration and raise funds. Furthermore, US engagement in the region has dramatically increased, indicated by a host of new bilateral cooperation arrangements, with Indonesia, Thailand, Singapore, Vietnam, and the Philippines. Therefore, to curb these illegal activities, the increase of defence expenditure among the countries of Southeast Asia is a natural choice.[36]

The Reaction of Regional Countries to the 9/11 Incident

The 9/11 attack and simultaneously, in the name of the Global War on Terrorism (GWOT), the launching of America's counter-attack on Osama Bin Laden's Al-Qaeda in Afghanistan, polarized the Southeast Asian nations. The US government had radically changed its views of Southeast Asian terrorism when its intelligence agencies unearthed various evidences linking terrorist groups in this region with Al-Qaeda.[37] Resultantly, the US policy makers viewed Southeast Asia as the major breeding ground for terrorism with the capability to inflict havoc not only against America but also against surrogate targets in Asia. Following this episode, Southeast Asian governments were vigilant in their retort against terrorism perpetuated by Muslim extremists considering the significant number of Muslim communities in the region, particularly in Indonesia, with its largest Muslim population in the world; in Malaysia, where Islam is embedded in the Constitution; and in Southern Philippines and Southern Thailand where some Muslim groups are fighting for separatism. While the countries of Southeast Asia declared their sympathy for US in the wake of the 9/11 incident, their willingness to become a part of the US initiated GWOT varied.[38] Indonesia and Malaysia spoke against the US-led retaliatory air strikes on Afghanistan, which they charged were killing innocent people (mainly Muslims) without dealing with terrorism. However, Singapore, the Philippines and Thailand, traditional American allies in this part of the world, were strong supporters of the US military forces in Afghanistan. This varied reaction was quite interesting in character.

The ASEAN Members' Initiative to Contain Terrorism in Southeast Asia

After the 9/11 incident, the problem of terrorism became an important agenda in many countries of Southeast Asia. Examining the effectiveness of counterterrorism measures is indeed a daunting task. Since September 2001, the US increased focus on the idea of Southeast Asia as a "second front"[39] in GWOT, on the ground of existence of radical Islamist and terrorist groups, particularly those in the Philippines, Indonesia, Malaysia, Thailand, and Singapore. Although, the countries of Southeast Asia, initially rejected the terrorist threats following the 9/11 incident, as pleaded by the US government, outlook drastically altered following the Bali Bombing in 2002. In spite of initial differences, respective countries' capacity to monitor, track down, and arrest suspected terrorists, evolved in the mindset to most of the members of

ASEAN in later years. They felt that ASEAN unity is more important to them than the war on terrorism and they needed to fight terrorism and related crimes through cooperation at the multilateral, regional and bilateral levels.

ASEAN, as a regional organisation has facilitated the development of legal and policy responses to terrorism in each member state in accordance with its foundational principles. However, differences have evolved among its members with reference to implementation of its various declarations and statements adopted, based on ASEAN principle of non-intervention, after the 9/11 incident, making implementation of its declarations and statements, less concrete and collective. Thus, regional cooperation to counter terrorism with reference to policy implementation among ASEAN members has been largely limited to bilateral and trilateral efforts. For example, Cambodia, Singapore, Indonesia and Brunei have adopted a comprehensive legislative approach to tackling the terrorist challenge, whereas Malaysia and Thailand have relied more on coercive, militaristic responses.

ASEAN's Brunei Declaration on Joint Action to Counter Terrorism

The ASEAN leaders addressed the issue of terrorism as a profound threat to international peace and security and "a direct challenge to the attainment of peace, progress and prosperity of ASEAN and the realisation of ASEAN Vision 2020". They expressed commitment to combat terrorism in accordance with the Charter of the UN, international laws and relevant UN resolutions and further mentioned "cooperative efforts in this regard should consider joint practical counter-terrorism measures in line with specific circumstances in the region and in each member country". Despite the limitation of ASEAN in addressing regional security threats, it still remains the core principal organisation in Southeast Asia tasked to tackle issues of regional cooperation to counter terrorism. Since 9/11 event, it has adopted several declarations and statements about the region's commitment to fight terrorism at the highest level and among them the 2001 ASEAN Declaration on Joint Action to Counter Terrorism (ADJACT), reached at the Seventh ASEAN Summit, held on 5 November 2001, at Brunei Darussalam, remained quite striking. In this meeting, the ASEAN Heads of State unequivocally condemned "in the strongest terms" the 9/11 2001 terrorist attacks in New York and Washington and considered such acts as an attack against humanity and an assault on "all of us." They viewed the acts of terrorism in all its forms and manifestations, committed wherever, whenever and by whomsoever, as a profound threat to international peace and security. They also rejected any attempt to link terrorism with any religion or race and committed to counter, prevent, and suppress all forms of terrorist acts in accordance with the UN Charter and other international laws, especially taking into account the importance of all relevant UN resolutions. Furthermore, the ASEAN members agreed to joint practical counterterrorism measures in line with specific circumstances in the region and in each member country. They also agreed on the practical steps to counter international terrorism, including review and strengthening of national mechanisms to combat international terrorism; early signing and/or ratification of or accession to all relevant anti-terrorism conventions including the International Convention for the Suppression of the Financing of Terrorism; deeper cooperation among front-line law enforcement agencies in combating terrorism and sharing "best practices"; enhanced information intelligence exchange to facilitate the flow of information, in particular, on terrorists and terrorist organisations, their movement and funding, and any other information needed to protect lives, property, and the security of all modes of travel; strengthened cooperation at bilateral, regional, and international levels in combating terrorism in a comprehensive manner affirming that at the international level, the UN should play a major role in this regard.[40] In this meeting, no operational coordination to seek out and hunt down terrorists operating cross-nationality was discussed, thereby once again revealing ASEAN's limitations as a security mechanism. For example, Philippines and Thailand had little reservations on the American bombing operations, while Indonesia and Malaysia called on the US to halt the bombing campaign. In fact, the ASEAN 'Declaration' on terrorism has been clearly a compromise statement in its final outcome.[41] Furthermore, in this meeting, the Philippine President Gloria Macapagal-Arroyo, in her keynote address, called for the formation of a five-country coalition plan to battle terrorist activities in the region and proposed that Indonesia, Malaysia, Singapore, Thailand and the Philippines would share intelligence information, conduct joint border patrols and possibly forge a peace-keeping force in order to improve cooperation among their law enforcement agencies and suggested that the ASEAN should pursue broader inter-faith dialogues to promote solidarity among Christians, Muslims, Buddhists and members of other religions.[42] Thus, the 2001 ADJACT remained a milestone event in the annals of ASEAN history.

The above-mentioned explicit resolutions have been incorporated in the Terrorism Component of the Work Programme to Implement the ASEAN

Plan of Action to Combat Transnational Crime, adopted in May 2002. It is based on six strategic thrusts: information exchange; cooperation in legal matters; cooperation in law enforcement matters; institutional capacity building; training; and extra-regional cooperation. Following the Brunei Summit, the ASEAN meeting at Phuket, Thailand in February 2002 focused on terrorism and tried to counter the image that Southeast Asia was a haven for terrorists. The Malaysian Foreign Minister wanted arrests of terrorists to be viewed as "a credit, not a debit," i.e. he wanted ASEAN states to be seen as partners in the war on terrorism, not targets. The Philippines, Indonesia and Malaysia drafted an agreement for intelligence sharing, synchronisation of investigation methods and extradition; to strengthen each other's capacity to arrest suspected terrorists. Thailand wanted to examine the details before it would sign it. But no agreement was signed, and no formal statement issued except to declare a "New Era" in the War on Terrorism.[43] Following the 2001 ADJACT agreement, Malaysia, Indonesia and the Philippines on 7 May 2002 at Putrajaya, Malaysia, signed a trilateral agreement to increase cooperation by the three governments to address cross-border incidents and transnational crimes. The agreement called for border controls and sharing of information on airline passenger lists, and agreed for joint training exercises, set up of hot lines, standard search-and-rescue procedures, and sharing of intelligence. Furthermore, the three countries also agreed to fight "any persons or groups out to terrorise people or threaten or harm them, expose the environment or endanger national resources or international facilities, or threaten the stability, territorial integrity, political unity or sovereignty of independent states."[44] At the end of this meeting, the Philippine President contended that the pact is more of an "operational agreement" rather than a treaty to help the three countries fight terrorism in their common seas.

ASEAN's Unified Plan to Combat Terrorism

Meanwhile, on 17 May 2002, the ASEAN countries agreed on a unified plan of action to combat terrorism and adopted the "Work Programme to Implement the ASEAN Plan of Action to Combat Transnational Crime." The plan focused on eight priority areas "illicit drug trafficking, arms smuggling, trafficking of women and children, piracy, international economic crime, cyber crime, money laundering and terrorism". The ASEAN member countries agreed to work towards the harmonisation of laws among members in order to effectively deal with the issues of transnational crime and decided to develop programmes for joint exercises and simulations in various areas to enhance cooperation and coordination in law enforcement and intelligence sharing.

Following this meeting, a two-day special ASEAN Ministerial Meeting on Terrorism was held in Kuala Lumpur from 20-21 May, 2002. At the end of this meeting, the ASEAN countries agreed to the possibility of working together towards having a common legislation to fight terrorism in the region. The ASEAN members also agreed to recognise the right of individual member countries to continue pursuing practical preventive measures to address the root cause of terrorism and to obey the sovereignty, territorial integrity and domestic laws of each member country in order to uphold the fight against terrorism. A 16-point communiqué, published at the end of this meeting, clearly outlined ASEAN's efforts to counter, prevent and suppress all forms of terrorist acts in accordance with the UN Charter and other international laws. ASEAN also reaffirmed its commitment and support to undertake the fight against acts of terrorism committed wherever, whenever and by whomsoever without discrimination and with due respect to religion, race, culture and nationality.[45] Finally, at the end of this meeting, the ASEAN members agreed to the possibility of working together towards having a common legislation to fight terrorism in the region and agreed to establish the Regional Counter-terrorism Centre in November 2002 in Kuala Lumpur. After this meeting, on 29 November 2004, the ASEAN members signed an agreement relevant to its counterterrorism efforts—the Treaty on Mutual Legal Assistance in Criminal Matters, known as the Mutual Legal Assistance Treaty (MLAT). The core aim of the MLAT was to enhance the effectiveness of the law enforcement agencies of ASEAN member states in the investigation and prosecution of offences through co-operation and mutual legal assistance in criminal matters. In 2005, a two-year basis to maintain its relevance and adequacy in responding to the changing nature of transnational crime and to include the provisions of the Vientiane Action Programme (VAP), a six-year guideline towards the establishment of an ASEAN Community had been adopted. Since then, more than a dozen regional counter-terrorism projects have been developed, ranging from "hard" law enforcement measures, such as developing region-wide border control mechanism to prevent terrorist movements to "soft" rehabilitative programmes aimed at reintegrating "reformed" terrorist to the mainstream society.

On 13 January 2007, the ASEAN Convention on Counter-Terrorism (ACCT) took place at Cebu, Philippines. In this convention, "the Charter of the United Nation and relevant principles of international law, the relevant international conventions and protocols relating to counterterrorism and relevant resolutions of the United Nations on measures aimed at countering international terrorism, and reaffirming our commitment to protect human rights, fair treatment, the rule of law, and due process as well as the principles enshrined in the Treaty of Amity and Cooperation in Southeast Asia done at Bali on 24 February 1976" has been recalled and it was reaffirmed that "terrorism cannot and should not be associated with any religion, nationality, civilisation or ethnic group" and thereby provided the much needed framework to lay out specific practical measures and to ensure its full implementation.[46] However, as a legally binding instrument, the ACCT aims at deepening cooperation among the enforcement agencies of its member nations in counterterrorism and provides a framework for regional cooperation to counter, prevent and suppress terrorism in all its forms and could be described as 'an important milestone in ASEAN counter-terrorism co-operation with much potential in the areas of information-sharing and capacity-building'. An interesting point to be noted in this context, that the ACCT achieved its full ratification only in 2013-six years after it was signed, although it came into force in 2011 after the sixth ASEAN member state had ratified it. As a continuation of early resolutions in 2015, there was a special ministerial meeting to respond to the rise of radicalisation and violent extremism. Recently in 2016, ASEAN Foreign Ministers announced the statement regarding terrorist attack in Jakarta. From this timeline, ASEAN is still having problem in conducting a common policy. They took time to ratify the convention and apply the real action, while the terrorists could have planned their agendas. Besides this, the countries of Southeast Asia have signed joint agreements with a number of countries, like, the United States, the European Union (EU), Australia, India, Russia, Japan, the Republic of Korea, New Zealand, Pakistan and Canada, etc., in order to contain the issue of terrorism. Thus, with these ASEAN resolutions to counterterrorism, the countries of Southeast Asia have temporarily adjusted to the unusual situation arising out of the 9/11 tragedy.

Major Constraints in Implementing the ASEAN Counterterrorism Measures

Although, the ASEAN members have explored numerous frameworks to facilitate regional cooperation to counter terrorism through varying combinations of approaches, like, military measures; socio-economic issues, ideological, and educational policies, as well as the enactment and enforcement of counter-terrorism laws, locally, regionally and internationally, unfortunately this organisation remains scrawny in implementing these resolutions and have incredible problems in fulfilling this because of national sensitivities. Though regional counterterrorism teamwork within ASEAN has improved since 9/11, countering terrorism at the operational level is not yet well coordinated and is ad hoc in nature "due to the constraints of conflicting national interests and mutual suspicions." Furthermore, the unresolved bilateral tensions "have stymied security cooperation at both bilateral and multilateral levels."[47] In the context of diverse threat perceptions and the nucleus of ASEAN principles of sovereignty and non-interference, the members had "great incentive to be cautious and view the problem of terrorism in terms of domestic, not region wide, implications."[48] This resulted in a problem with implementation of the ASEAN resolutions as they differ from one ASEAN member to another, on account of ASEAN principle of non-intervention and maintenance of sovereignty, which governs inter-state relationships. Therefore, the regional counterterrorism approach is primarily built on the lowest ordinary denominator and vulnerable base and largely inspired by respective country's emphasis more on domestic interest rather than regional viewpoint. So, ASEAN's counterterrorism policies often reflect the state- and regime-centric view of security and for that it cannot move beyond the mandate of the member states.

It is true that in all counties of Southeast Asia, the issue of terrorism is not uniform in nature and each government handled it according to their own domestic necessity. For example, Indonesia, Cambodia, Brunei, and Singapore have adopted a comprehensive legislative approach to tackle the challenge; whereas Malaysia, the Philippines and Thailand depend more on coercive and militaristic means. The Government of **Philippines** immediately after the 9/11 episode, under the leadership of Gloria Macapagal-Arroyo, branded the Abu Sayyaf Group as an international terrorist movement and accepted from the US a significant military aid package and direct military assistance to counter Abu Sayyaf Group fighters on Basilan Island and which in fact gave an opportunity to reduce its long-drawn internal tension.[49] Likewise, both **Brunei** and **Singapore** endorsed legislation to combat financing of terrorism upon their attainment to or ratification of the Terrorist Financing Convention in 2002. However, no further counterterrorism measure was adopted until they ratified the ACCT in 2011 and 2007 respectively. The Singapore government granted the 1997 Terrorist Bombing Convention only in 2007 and in the same year enacted the Terrorism (Suppression of Bombings) Act 2007, in order to give effect to the 1997 Convention. Similarly, Brunei ratified its comprehensive counterterrorism legislation on 1 August 2011 soon after its ratification of the ACCT on 28 April 2011, even though it acceded to the 1997 Convention much earlier in 2002.[50] **Malaysia**, while stressing terrorism financing as part of their anti-money laundering policy, which was consistent with ASEAN's outlook to regional co-operation against transnational crime and endorsed the Anti-Money Laundering, Anti-Terrorism Financing and Proceeds of Unlawful Activities Act 2001 (Malaysia), with a view to implementing obligations under the relevant UN Security Council resolutions provides a comprehensive and effective legal framework to combat terrorism[51] and in July 2003, it had established a Southeast Asia Regional Centre for Counterterrorism, with the prime mission of regional training, information sharing and public awareness campaigns. Similarly, **Thailand's** counterterrorism outlook was intended to repress separatist movements in the southern Malay-Muslim provinces. This has become more institutionalised with the enactment of Thailand's Internal Security Act of 2008.[52]

However, unlike the founding members of ASEAN, the development of anti-terror security outlook and corresponding legal instruments did not appear to be an imperative priority for newer member states. For **Cambodia**, while the policy emphasis has been on transnational crime, it has looked towards Australia and US for help in order to develop its counterterrorism capability. Similarly, **Vietnam** commenced the process of developing programs to implement the provisions of the ACCT upon ratification in 2010, including the enactment of counterterrorism specific legislation. Although it did not have to deal with terrorism in any significant way, Lao People's Democratic Republic established a National Ad Hoc Committee for implementing Security Council Resolution 1373, and amended its penal law in 2005 to criminalise various acts of terrorism.[53] Finally, **Myanmar** has been working with the International Monetary Fund and the UN Office on Drugs and Crime in drafting its counterterrorism and anti-money laundering laws pursuant to Security Council Resolution 1373 and Resolution 1624, while seeking assistance from the US and international organisations for the capacity building of its Financial Intelligence Unit that oversees terrorist financing issues. Along with this, the Myanmar government introduced the *Control of Money Laundering Law 2002* (Myanmar), with a view to implementing obligations under the relevant UN Security Council resolutions. While maintaining the official position that the existing criminal law provides a comprehensive and effective legal framework to combat terrorism.[54] Thus, the above-mentioned outlook clearly exhibits that these internal political and legal means have limited

ASEAN's capacity to harmonise its counterterrorism measures into a comprehensive one.

Therefore, in a nutshell, the counterterrorism legal instruments hitherto adopted by the members of ASEAN can be termed as 'squashy laws', whose core aim has been to present an overarching framework through which the respective and varied counter-terrorism policies of the ASEAN member countries could be synchronised, as well as to secure region-wide support. In a region, where the principle of non-interference governs interstate relationship, this squashy approach to regional co-operation on counterterrorism faces numerical hurdles. However, this does not necessarily mean that ASEAN is in any way restrained in exercising its institutional competence to facilitate the development and domestic implementation of legal responses to terrorism through regional cooperation.

Challenges to ASEAN Principle of Non-Intervention

In the last five decades, ASEAN's institutional competence has arguably been exercised in accordance with its longstanding principles of respect for state sovereignty and non-interference, serving simply to harmonise national and sub-regional efforts. Over the years, ASEAN's principles of non-interference and non-use of force have maintained regional stability by liberating member nations from the threat of interference from their neighbours, leaving them free to address domestic issues of political and economic stability and development. Therefore, the regional counter-terrorism teamwork through ASEAN is designed, as discussed above, to be complementary to respective national efforts to counter modern transnational terrorist threats by providing necessary opportunities to trounce the limits of national efforts. The Declaration of ASEAN Concord II – known as the Bali Concord II – which was held on 7-8 October, 2003, at Bali in the Ninth ASEAN Summit, sets out the vision of an ASEAN Community clearly affirming the fundamental principles governing ASEAN cooperation, which include: non-interference and respect for national sovereignty, the renunciation of the threat or the use of force, and peaceful settlement of differences and disputes.[55] This preservation of sovereignty principle is further reiterated in the newly-ratified ASEAN Charter, despite discourses about 'diluting' it prior to and during this draft.

Actually, the maintenance of this 'sovereignty' concept primarily originated from the framework of TAC, signed in February 1976 at Bali by the then ASEAN members. This treaty was aimed at promoting perpetual peace, everlasting amity and cooperation among their people, which would contribute to their strength, solidarity and closer relationship. Article 2 of the TAC clearly stresses the principle of "mutual respect for the independence, sovereignty, equality, territorial integrity and national identity of all nations." It also highlights "the right of every state to lead its national existence free from external interference, subversion or coercion." Most prominently the TAC enshrines the principle of non-interference in the internal affairs of one another.[56] However, important changes in certain areas of international relations require a reassessment of such a principle, especially when the domestic problems of one state have far-reaching effects pervading the borders of neighbouring states. On many occasions, this internal domestic unrest of one country poses a serious challenge to the peace and stability of the region.

Meanwhile, in the mid-1990s, on account of certain intra and inter-state problems among the ASEAN members, led Thailand's Foreign Minister Surin Pitsuwanto challenge ASEAN's cardinal 'principle of non-intervention' and called for a change in the ASEAN's Foreign Ministers meeting held in June 1998 at Manila. He demanded that the ASEAN members be allowed to openly discuss each other's domestic affairs and dubbed his proposal as "constructive intervention". He said: "The principle of non-intervention is not the real issue ... the real issue is how we can work together in dealing with the new challenges of a new millennium."[57] This proposal of Surin Pitsuwan received the support of the Philippines government, but ultimately was rejected by rest of ASEAN members, who advocated "constructive interventions" in certain regional issues and emphasised the essentiality of the retention of the principle of non-intervention, on the ground of "practical" necessity without which ASEAN cannot stay relevant to address the local, regional and international challenges. Therefore, the challenges that have been confronting ASEAN are due to the ambivalence on the part of its member states towards rigorous counter-terrorism measures because of domestic political reasons, as much as the legal and political constraints upon ASEAN. National counterterrorism efforts in each country are enmeshed in their own political agenda of national harmony and combating dissidents. The ASEAN members are too cautious in their approach in regional counter terrorism measures in order to maintain ASEAN solidarity, which, to a certain extent, constrains the effectiveness of regional initiatives in the region. The relevant question is, therefore, to what extent ASEAN has contributed to the development and implementation of counter-terrorism law and policy through its exercise of institutional competence to address a shared security interest? In reality, the fact remains that counterterrorism in Southeast Asia rests on the capacity of individual members to act. Inter-state coordination against terrorism remains voluntary and non-binding. This naturally limits the role of ASEAN to actually address terrorist threats in the region. ASEAN's stand against terrorism has not moved beyond the level of political rhetoric because of the perpetual absence of strong institutional framework to implement its principles. However, these differing levels of political will and the different capabilities to effectively combat terrorism in the Southeast Asian region cannot be branded as a feeble regional exercise, but an exercise with sincere motives, based on regional cohesion and long-drawn outlook to overcome the menace of terrorism in emerging global scenario. The fact remains that after all, the principles of an organisation are the reflection of a region's unique character, beliefs and history.

The Recent ISIS Incidents in Southeast Asia

The emergence of Islamic State in Iraq and Syria (ISIS) and its terrorist activities have established an impact on the turf of Southeast Asia. The recent ISIS-aligned group attacks in Jakarta on January 14 (2016), the April 9 (2016) attack on Philippine security forces in the southern island of Basilan conducted by groups claiming allegiance to ISIS, and the wave of kidnappings in southern Philippines clearly exhibit the recurrence of threat of terrorism in the domain of Southeast Asian countries. Since mid-2014, the Southeast Asian dimension of ISIS was given something of a formal expression with the formation of Katibah Nusantara, a Southeast Asian wing of ISIS formed by Malay and Indonesian speaking fighters in Syria. This Katibah fulfills several functions and among them, it provides a social network to help Southeast Asian recruits settle, training for those among them who would eventually take up arms, and communicate with the network of pro-ISIS groups operating in Syria. Indonesia remains the victim of the first ISIS-inspired attack in Southeast Asia. This event occurred on January 14 (2016), when self-proclaimed followers of ISIS set off bombs at a Starbucks outside the Sarinah mall and at a nearby police outpost, and gunfire broke out on the streets at Jalan Tamrin in the heart of Jakarta.[58] Regional governments appear quite vigilant to this ISIS-related developments, particularly in terms of monitoring both returnees as well as communications between militants in Syria and their counterparts and followers back home. As a result, once again the countries of Southeast Asia draw attention and re-accelerated the past strategies which emanated with this re-surfacing threat in terms of counterterrorism strategies, narratives, and cooperation. The effort to tackle the growing presence of ISIS should not be separated from its efforts to counter the decades' long terrorist threat facing this region. While ASEAN as a regional organisation has made a number of initiatives to counter such terrorist threats, it should learn from the major shortcomings and failures of the past years to address the threats of ISIS. Moreover, it is important to note that ASEAN members must ensure a common approach to countering terrorism and avoid narrow national interests or political concerns in the interest of regional cohesion.

Conclusion: The Space for Renewed Regional Policy Discourse

From the above discussion, it is clear that efforts to counter the threat of terrorism within the framework of ASEAN have been met by a number of challenges, which practically limit its capability at the regional level, making their counterterrorism initiatives occasionally less effective and ethereal. The core flaws of the ASEAN countries' role emerge from the lack of regional willing/unwilling mindset towards combating terrorism, different approaches in addressing terrorism among its member-states, unwilling mindset to ratify ASEAN efforts to counter terrorism, severe differences regarding addressing this issue, i.e. between transnational and domestic debate, lack of political will and the question of national sovereignty. This resulted in that ASEAN cooperation to counter terrorism is still in its embryonic forms. As such it was geared more towards building-up the law-enforcement capacity to counter terrorism at the regional level. Yet, over the years, terrorism in Southeast Asia has remained more local than global and its process of implementing counterterrorism measures is inadequate in its entirety. It is a fact that ASEAN members' strong assertion of the principle of non-interference in each other's internal affairs in a transformed era often acts as a stumbling block for effective anti-terror cooperation. To address this issue dynamically, ASEAN should adopt a more pro-active role—a role quite different from the basis upon which the regional grouping has proceeded using the "ASEAN Way". Dialogue-based approaches to conflict mitigation through a combination of 'hard' and 'soft' security policies could be a better way to mitigate this problem. Moreover, it must not treat terrorist threat as a battle between Islam and terrorism. However, in spite of these weaknesses, it is a fact that the issue of terrorism has been able to generate a broad general consensus among member states and the security cooperation has been really noteworthy. It is true that ASEAN has proved to become a 'pioneer' in reconciling the intra-state and inter-state dynamics that shape terrorist threats, counterterrorism policies and overall regional cohesion.

The outcome of its balancing approach will have a decisive impact on ASEAN's quest for realising a more tangible community building process. If successful, it will showcase ASEAN as a model for similar quests in other developing regions to apply counter-terrorism as an instrument of successful regional integration.[59] Hence, a mix of passion, persuasion, perseverance, agility, negotiation and diplomacy could be regarded as a suitable method to resolve this decades' old unceasing problem. Only then can the problem of terrorism be dealt with more efficiently and in a skillful way, and thereby generate peace and regional stability, which have existed in the social fabric of the Southeast Asian countries over the years.

NOTES

1 Gus Martin, *Understanding Terrorism: Challenges, Perspectives and Issues,* Sage Publications, London and California, 2003, pp.1–10

2 See Terrorism Research Center, http://www.terrorism.com/. (accessed on 22 January, 2017)

3 For details see Center for the Study of Terrorism and Political Violence, at http://www.standrews. ac.uk/~wwwir/research/cstpv/index.php. (accessed on 22 January, 2017)

4 For details see Center on Global Counterterrorism Cooperation at http://www.globalct.org. (accessed on 22 January, 2017)

5 Cited in Carlyle A. Thayer, "Political Terrorism and Militant Islam in Southeast Asia," (Paper delivered at a Forum on Regional Security and Political Developments, organized by the Institute of Southeast Asian Studies at Grand Copthorne Water Front Hotel, Singapore on 24 July, 2003), p. 6.

6 The principal groups that had signed ceasefire agreements include the United Wa State Army (UWSA), the Shan State Army (SSA), the Kachin Independence Army (KIA), and the Karenni National Progressive Party (KNPP). At present, there are only a handful of active ethnic insurgent movements that could realistically pose any concerted threat to the Myanmar Government. Among these, the most prominent are the Karen National Union (KNU) and the Shan United Revolutionary Army (SURA).

7 Peter Chalk, "Separatism and Southeast Asia: The Islamic Factor in Southern Thailand, Mindanao and Aceh", *Studies in Conflict and Terrorism*, Vol. 24, No. 4, July-August 2001, pp.241–42

8 Clive Christie, *A Modern History of Southeast Asia: Decolonization, Nationalism and Separatism,* Tauris Academic Studies, London, 1996, p.192.

9 For detailed discussion, see Rohan Gunaratna (ed), The Changing Face of Terrorism, Marshall Cavendish International, Singapore, 2004; Andrew Tan and Kumar Ramakrishna (eds), The New Terrorism: Anatomy, Trends and Counter-Strategies, Marshall Cavendish International, Singapore, 2002. Also see Walter Laqueur, *No End to War: Terrorism in the Twenty-First Century*, The Continuum International Publishing Group, Inc., New York and London, 2003 and Ian O. Lesser, Bruce Hoffman, John Arquilla, David Ronfeldt

and Michele Zanimi, *Countering the New Terrorism,* California: RAND, Santa Monica, 1999.

10 Andrew T.H. Tan, "Terrorism and Insurgency in Southeast Asia" in Andrew T.H. Tan (ed), *A Handbook of Terrorism and Insurgency in Southeast Asia,* Edward Elgar Publishing, Inc., Great Britain and Massachusetts, 2007, p.5, also see Linell Cady and Sheldon Simon (eds), *Religion and Conflicts in South and Southeast Asia: Disrupting Violence,* Routledge: London and New York, 2007, and S. Yunanto, et. al, *Militant Islamic Movements in Indonesia and Southeast Asia* Friedrich-Ebert Stiftung, Jakarta, 2003

11 Carlyle Thayer, "New Terrorism in Southeast Asia" in Damien Kingburry (ed), *Violence in Between: Conflict and Security in Archipelagic Southeast Asia,* Monash University Press and Institute of Southeast Asian Studies, Victoria and Singapore, 2005, pp. 53–74

12 For a thorough analysis on Al-Qaeda, see Jane Corbin, Al-Qaeda: *The Terror Network That Threatens the World,* Thunder's Mouth Press, New York, 2002

13 For details see *Rohan Gunaratna, Inside Al-Qaeda: Global Network of Terror,* Columbia University Press, New York, 2002; Maria Ressa, *Seeds of Terror: An Eyewitness Account of Al-Qaeda's Newest Center of Operations in Southeast Asia,* Free Press, New York and London, 2003

14 *Rohan Gunaratna, Inside Al-Qaeda: Global Network of Terror,* Columbia University Press, New York, 2002, p.175

15 See Zachary Abuza, *Militant Islam in Southeast Asia: Crucible of Terror,* Lynne Rienner Publishers, Inc., Boulder, Colorado, 2003

16 *Ibid,* p.1

17 "Counter Terrorism Measures in Southeast Asia: How Effective Are They?", Rommel C. Banlaoi, Yuchengco Center, De La Salle University, Manila, 2009, p.15

18 Andrew T.H. Tan, "Terrorism and Insurgency in Southeast Asia" in Andrew T.H. Tan (ed), A Handbook of Terrorism and Insurgency in Southeast Asia, Edward Elgar Publishing, Inc., Great Britain and Massachusetts, 2007, pp.11–13

19 Tridib Chakraborti, "Terrorism and the ASEAN States: A Classificatory and Prescriptive Analysis," in Omprakash Mishra and Sucheta Ghosh (eds.), *Terrorism and low Intensity Conflict in South Asian Region,* Manak Publications Pvt. Ltd., New Delhi, 2003, pp.319–32

20 See US Department of State, "List of Foreign Terrorist Organizations" at http://www.state.gov/s/ct/list/ (accessed on 16 December, 2016).

21 "Terrorism in Southeast Asia", Congressional Research Service, 16 October, 2009, p.2, see www.crs.gov (accessed on 22 December, 2016)

22 *Ibid.*, p. 3

23 Mohammed Jawhar Hassan, "Terrorism: Southeast Asia's Response," PacNet Newsletters, No. 1-4 January, 2002

24 Tridib Chakraborti, n.19, pp.341–42

25 For detailed Communiqué of the 29th ASEAN Ministerial Meeting in Jakarta, July 1996, see, https://cil.nus.edu.sg/rp/pdf/1996%20Joint%20Communique% 20of%20 The % 2029th%20ASEAN%20Ministerial%20Meeting-pdf.pdf, p.10 (accessed on 22 January, 2017)

26 See http://asean.org/?static_post=asean-declaration-on-transnational-crime-manila-20-december-1997, pp.1–2 (accessed on 16 December, 2016)

27 See https://www.mfa.gov.sg/content/dam/mfa/images/om/UN_new_york/AnnexG.pdf, pp. 1–4 (accessed on 16 December, 2016)

28 Tridib Chakraborti, n.19, p.341

29 Peter Rosendorff and Tod Sandler, "The Political Economy of Transnational Terrorism," Journal of Conflict Resolution, Vol. 49, No. 2, April 2005, p. 171

30 For detailed analysis, see INDONESIA Briefing Jakarta/Brussels, 24 October 2002, International Crisis Group, at https://www.files.ethz.ch/isn/28151/b023_bali_ bombings.pdf (accessed on 22 January, 2017)

31 Zaff S. Solmerin, "Armed Conflicts Displaced 150,000 Folks," *Asian Tribune*, 21 November, 2002, at http://www.asiantribune.com/oldsite/show_news.php?id=1228 (accessed on 22 January, 2017)

32 International Displacement Monitoring Centre, "International Displacement in Asia and the Pacific" at http://www.internal-displacement.org/ (accessed on 22 January, 2017)

33 See Rommel C. Banlaoi, "Counter Terrorism Measures in Southeast Asia: How Effective Are They?" Yuchengco Center, De La Salle University, Manila, Philippines, 2009, p.71, at http://www.academia.edu/1833307/Counter_Terrorism_Measures_in_ Southeast_Asia_How_Effective_Are_They_by_Rommel_Banlaoi (accessed on 16 December, 2016)

34 See Heda Bayron, "Southeast Asian Nations Increasing Spending on Defense," Voice of Asia News, 17 July, 2002, at http://www.voanews.com/english/archive/2002-07/a-2002-07-17-2-Southeast.cfm?moddate=2002-07-17 (accessed on 22 January, 2017).

35 For details see Eric Heginbotham, "The fall and rise of navies in East Asia: military organizations, domestic politics, and grand strategy", *International Security*, Vol.27, No.2, 2002, pp.86–125; also see *Asia Times*, 'Malacca Strait: target for terror', 11 August 2004, at http://www.atimes.com/atimes/Southeast Asia/FH11Ae02.html (accessed on 25 January, 2017)

36 For details see S. Narayan, "Economic Impact of Terrorism on the Southeast Asian Region", ISAS Insights No. 8, 25 October 2005, Institute of South Asian Studies, Singapore, at https://www.files.ethz.ch/isn/23835/8.pdf (accessed on 22 January, 2017)

37 See Rommel C. Banlaoi, n.33, p. 24,

38 For details see Sheldon W. Simon, "Mixed Reactions in Southeast Asia to the US War on Terrorism," Comparative Connections: An E-Journal on East Asian Bilateral Relations, 4th Quarter, 2001, p. 1

39 For details see John Gershman, "Is Southeast Asia the Second Front?" *Foreign Affairs* July/August, 2002

40 For details see Association of Southeast Asian Nations (ASEAN): Treaties and Regimes,31 January, 2017, The ASEAN Secretariat, Jakarta, Indonesia, at http://www.nti.org//learn/treaties-and- regimes/association-southeast-asian-nations-asean/ (accessed on 24 January, 2017)

41 *The Hindu*, 6 November 2002.

42 Tridib Chakraborti, n.19, pp. 350–51

43 Tridib Chakraborti, n.19, p. 351

44 For details see http://www.ops.gov.ph/malaythai2002news3.htm. (accessed on 17 January, 2017)

45 For details see http://www.aseansec.org/view.asp?file=/newdata/ sammter.htm, pp.1-3 (accessed on 19 January, 2017)

46 For details see https://cil.nus.edu.sg/2007/2007-asean-convention-on-counter-terrorism-signed-on-13-january-2007-in-cebu-philippines-by-the-heads-of-stategovernment/ (accessed on 16 January, 2017)

47 Tan, Andrew T.H. "The New Terrorism: How Southeast Asia Can Counter It?" in Uwe Johannen, Alan Smith and James Gomez (eds), 9/11: September 11 & Political Freedom: Asian Perspectives, Select Publishing, Pvt., Ltd, Singapore, 2003, p.7, cited in Rommel C. Banlaoi, n.39, p.94

48 J.T. Chow, "ASEAN Counterterorrism Cooperation since 9/11", *Asian Survey,* Vol. 45, No.2, 2000, p. 320

49 For details, see, Larry Niksch, "Abu Sayyaf: Target of Philippine–US Anti-Terrorism Cooperation", Congress Research Service, United States Congress, 24 January 2007, athttps://www.fas.org/sgp/crs/terror/RL31265.pdf (accessed on 19 January, 2017).

50 Seng Tan and Hitoshi Nasu, "ASEAN and the Development of Counter-Terrorism Law and Policy in Southeast Asia", *Thematic,* The University of New South Wales Law Journal, Vol. 39, No. 3, 2016, p. 1232, http://www.unswlawjournal.unsw.edu.au/sites/default/files/393-13.pdf (accessed on 22 January, 2017); For more analysis also see, Michael Hor, 'Singapore's Anti-Terrorism Laws: Reality and Rhetoric' in Victor V Ramraj et.al. (eds), *Global Anti-Terrorism Law and Policy,* Cambridge University Press, 2nd edition, 2012, pp, 271 and 284–5.

51 Seng Tan and Hitoshi Nasu, "ASEAN and the Development of Counter-Terrorism Law and Policy in Southeast Asia", *Thematic,* The University of New South Wales Law Journal, Vol. 39, No. 3, 2016, p. 1231, at http://www.unswlawjournal.unsw.edu.au/sites/default/files/393-13.pdf (accessed on 22 January, 2017)

52 *Ibid.*

53 For detailed discussion see *Ibid,* pp.1231–32

54 *Ibid,* pp. 1233 and 1231

55 For Declaration of ASEAN Concord II (Bali Concord II) See http://asean.org/?static_post=declaration-of-asean-concord-ii-bali-concord-ii (accessed on 22 January, 2017)

56 ASEAN: An Overview, ASEAN Secretariat, Jakarta, 1995, p.56.

57 Daljit Singh, "Southeast Asian in 1999: A False Dawn?", Southeast Asian Affairs : 2000, Institute of Southeast Asian Studies, Singapore, 2000, p.6.

58 Sidney Jones, "Battling ISIS in Indonesia," *New York Times,* January 18, 2016.

59 SartikaSoesilowati, "ASEAN's Response to the Challenge of Terrorism", Tahun 2011, Vol. 24, No. 3, p.240, at http://journal.unair.ac.id/filerPDF/06%20sartika%20jurnal%20MKP %20terorismenew%20_tyas_%20_editan%20niken_.pdf (accessed on 25 January, 2017)

7

Internal Armed Conflicts

Nitin A. Gokhale

Internal Threats and Internal Disturbances

Serious internal threats to the security of a nation state usually of the state evolve over a period of time. Often, during this tortuous process, government indifference, ambivalence, procrastination, inappropriate action and repressive over-reaction can worsen the situation.

Internal threats cause internal disturbances that manifest in either one or a combination of the following ways—civil disturbances, subversion, insurgency and civil war. But, it is the complex issue of "new terrorism" that casts its shadow over them all.

Terrorism

Terror in the socio-political and security context is a tool, a weapon, a tactic. It is a means used to instil extreme fear in the minds of a target audience, i.e. civil society and/or the government: to undermine it and to coerce it into submitting to the demands of the perpetrators. Terror is often referred to as "armed propaganda" and "propaganda of the deed". It is "a potent form of persuasion," a form of violent subversion.

A terrorist act is defined by the nature of the act. It is neither defined by the cause for which the act is committed nor is it defined by the identity of the perpetrators of the act. It has several distinguishing characteristics. It is typically carried out by an organised group against non-combatants. It seeks publicity and is usually motivated by ideological, political and/or religious reasons. Recent attempts to expand the scope of the term to include acts against military targets under specific conditions, for example hostage taking in peace and non-conflict areas, serve only to weaken the moral opprobrium attached otherwise to acts of terror.

Simply put, a terrorist act is a violent criminal act against non-combatants to influence an audience beyond the victims of the attack. The term terrorist applies to a person who perpetrates a terrorist act. The person may be domestic or international. In general, the term is reserved for non-state actors including those who are indulged in by states that sponsor terrorism.

In 2003, the Supreme Court of India had referred to Schmidt proposal of 1992 describing terrorism as "Act of Terrorism = Peacetime Equivalent of War Crime." This indeed had been proposed by Schmidt of the UN Crime Branch in 1992. In 2002, the European Union had come up with the definition, "Given their nature or context, [acts which] may seriously damage a country or an international organisation where committed with the aim of seriously intimidating a population." Eventually in 2005, the UNGA defined terrorism as, "Criminal acts intended or calculated to provoke a state of terror in the general public, a group of persons or particular persons for political purposes are in any circumstance unjustifiable, whatever the considerations of a political, philosophical, ideological, racial, ethnic, religious or any other nature that may be invoked to justify them." Interestingly, Saudi Arabia Terrorism Law of 2014 even includes individual act against an individual project (Hate Crimes?) by saying, "Any act carried out by an offender in furtherance of an individual or collective project, directly or indirectly, intended to disturb the public order of the state, or to shake the security of society, or the stability of the state, or to expose its national unity to danger, or to suspend the basic law of governance or some of its articles, or to insult the reputation of the state or its position, or to inflict damage upon one of its public utilities or its natural resources, or to attempt to force a governmental authority to carry out or prevent it from carrying out an action, or to threaten to carry out acts that lead to the named purposes or incite [these acts]."

Whilst dictatorships may use terror to "discipline" society, in a democracy to describe instruments of state that may be guilty of errant conduct-human rights violations and the disproportionate use of force-as terrorists; and their actions as "state terror" is inappropriate. Such acts do not aim at destabilising civil society and the state. On the other hand, they do constitute a serious breach of domestic law and must be dealt with accordingly.

Whereas the terms terror, terrorist act and terrorist are relatively easy to explain and understand, the term terrorism is confusing. Even the United Nations has failed to arrive at a universal definition of the term. Unfortunately, consensus on the issue is unlikely as long as states: (a) support and sponsor acts of terror in other countries; and (b) gloss over the criminal and terrorist activities of insurgents and "freedom fighters." The absence of an agreed definition prevents reference to terrorism-related incidents in international courts. It allows countries to label any activity that they should choose to as terrorism, and it enables them to draw a parallel with such acts elsewhere to justify their own actions.

Nonetheless, terrorism is a global phenomenon that governments, individually and collectively will have to contend with, now and in the future; and the term is here to stay.

In the present circumstances, terrorism is perhaps best explained as the premeditated, systematic, and sustained use of terror as a strategy. It is distinct from individual and isolated acts of terror, howsoever violent.

Insurgency

Insurgency is the rise of armed force to bring about political change—"overthrow of the existing order": an armed rebellion. It is armed conflict below the level of conventional war. It combines political thought, the use of armed force, and popular support. Roger Trinquier famously refers to it as "modern warfare".

Conditions that favour an insurgency are a cause; a suitable physical environment; external support to include safe havens; and a weak government.

Both terrorism and subversion are embedded in insurgency and all three use violence for political purposes: yet they are distinct from each other. Terrorism and insurgency involve the premeditated use of armed force on scale which far exceeds the use of force in subversion.

Insurgency differs from terrorism in several other ways. Insurgency is a politico-military strategy whereas terrorism is a strategy based on the tactics of terror. Insurgents may possess an alternative vision and accept a compromise political solution whereas terrorists will not. Insurgents may resort to the use of several instruments, e.g. taxation, dispensation of justice; whereas terrorists have resort only to force and violence. Insurgents must enjoy popular support whereas such support is largely irrelevant to terrorists. Insurgency requires physical space and is predominantly a rural phenomenon, whereas terrorism, for the most part, is urban. Insurgent groups are relatively large, well organised and militarised, whereas terrorist groups are small and clandestine. Insurgents target the government and its instruments, whereas terrorists target non-combatants. Insurgents may hold territory, whereas terrorists do not.

Inevitably, government reactions to terrorism and insurgency are different too. Terrorism necessitates an "adversary-specific" response, aimed at destroying the terrorist organisation; while insurgency demands a "people-centric" approach aimed at securing the people and mobilising their support.

The term insurgency is frequently associated with a fight for a just cause—"freedom fighters in a freedom struggle." The term accords moral sanction and a measure of legitimacy to an insurgent movement. Whilst, in theory, armed rebels fighting for a cause should rightly be described as insurgents (or rebels), e.g. Mizo Insurgents, in practice, governments involved in internal armed conflict simply refuse to do so. They prefer to brand them as terrorists. Labelling subversives and insurgents as terrorists deprives them of the status they seek. And, there is justification for doing so: while all insurgents are not terrorists; all insurgencies do encompass terrorism. In law, dealing with terrorists and terrorism is simpler than dealing with insurgents and insurgency.

Insurgency invariably constitutes a serious threat to public order and security of the state, and can lead to civil war.

Internal disturbances—terrorism, civil disturbances, subversion, insurgency and civil war—pose a threat, varyingly, to law and order, public order and/or the security of the state. The government is compelled to respond to the threats to protect the individual, civil society and/or the state. The result is confrontation, conflict and, sometimes, armed conflict within the state—internal armed conflict.

Internal Armed Conflict

In a democracy, recourse to the use of force and violence against a government established and functioning in accordance with law is simply unacceptable—no matter what the reason or the provocation. The government is obliged to use all the legitimate means at its disposal, including the use of counter-force to respond appropriately to the threats.

The government's counter-force measures that correspond to the different types of internal threats and internal disturbances are counter-terrorism; the use of force to "disperse an unlawful assembly" during civil disturbances; counter-subversion; and counter-insurgency. All result in conflict that may or may not include the use of armed force but, not all constitute internal armed conflict.

Internal armed conflict is conflict that is confined to the territory of a single state wherein the intensity of violence exceeds levels normally associated with riots and isolated and sporadic acts involving the use of armed force. It implies the premeditated, organised, widespread and sustained use of armed force and violence by a group that threatens public order and/or the security of the state. It excludes civil disturbances and subversion, because of their relatively low levels of violence; as well as isolated acts of terror, because of their episodic nature.

Internal armed conflict is conflict at the lower end of the spectrum. In a sense, it is conflict "of the people, by the people, for the people". It pits the instruments of state against groups seemingly representing sections of the people of the state. Rupert Smith refers to it as "war amongst the people." It is an irregular, non-conventional, civil form of conflict. The causes of conflict, as indeed its solutions, invariably lie in the political, social and economic domain, i.e. outside the realm of the military. The people are the objective of the campaign. Political action is dominant and the use of force is restricted.

Pact on National Power

Internal armed conflict impacts adversely on peace, stability and tranquility within the state. It can hinder development, economic growth, progress and prosperity. At its worst it can threaten the very existence of the state. Internal armed conflicts can have a debilitating effect on the self-confidence and self-esteem of a nation. It can undermine national will and morale: both constituents of national power.

External Involvement

External involvement in internal armed conflict is not a new phenomenon. Domestic violence creates conditions that encourage intervention. A hostile power can either support or sponsor internal armed conflict. It may choose to intervene either covertly or clandestinely. This constitutes covert war. It is distinct from a surrogate or proxy war where a hostile state chooses to wage war through the government and instruments of a third country. Indeed, external involvement is deemed "crucial" in internal armed conflict.

Support may take several forms: political, diplomatic, moral and financial. It may be extended by state governments, non-governmental organisation and indigenous populations living abroad. Governments inimical to the victim state may also extend infrastructural, logistical, material that includes weapons, equipment and munitions, communications and training support.

In the 21st century, there are severe limitations to the conduct of conventional war between states. The influence of military power is declining: it is unable to resolve political, social and economic problems. Prohibitive financial and other costs and the low probability of decisive victory make war an unattractive option. The alteration of boundaries and the conquest and acquisition of territory through war is no longer acceptable: it does not enjoy moral sanction. And, the symmetry that the possession of weapons of mass destruction provides further diminishes its likelihood.

Under the circumstances, external involvement in internal armed conflict is an alternative to Inter-state war. The aggressor denies involvement and is careful not to cross the threshold of conventional war. A lack of evidence and the consequent inability of a victim state to garner the support of the international community can inhibit it from resorting to a conventional military response.

External involvement in internal armed conflict does not involve any overt commitment; it is prosecuted within the territory of the victim state; it is relatively economical and carries low risk. A RAND Corporation Report suggests that the support of an external power may help to accord recognition and legitimacy to a group or faction acting against the government, but cautions that such support can be a "mixed blessing". States supporting an insurgency are likely to have their own distinct political agenda; they may lend support to several groups simultaneously simply to keep their options open; and they may restrict the freedom of action of the groups they support.

External involvement in internal armed conflict is not necessarily a strategy of the weak. History is replete with examples of superpower involvement on the side of a group or faction acting against an incumbent government wielding power. Indeed, the US low-intensity conflict doctrine even prescribes support for insurgency. Internal armed conflict with external involvement and conventional general war differ in four fundamental ways—the nature of conflict, the objectives, the strategies, and the use of force. Firstly, internal armed conflict is an irregular, non-conventional, civil conflict: conventional war is a purely military contest. Secondly, in internal armed conflict, the people are the objective of the campaign: in conventional war, the objectives are territory and the armed forces of the enemy. Thirdly, internal armed conflict demands a joint civil-military strategy to resolve conflict: in conventional war, the war-fighting strategy is essentially military. And fourthly, in internal armed conflict the use of military force is self-regulated and restrained: in conventional war, the maximum possible use of force is made.

Early thinking on counter-insurgency accords primacy to the military for the destruction of the insurgent organisation and the control of the population. Subsequently, there is a discernible shift in emphasis. The people are the "centre of gravity". The population must be secured, protected, isolated from the insurgent and "mobilised"; political aspects and political reconciliation must be accorded priority; governments must function according to law; and adopt a "comprehensive" or "whole of government" approach.

Current Doctrine

British Army doctrine, influenced by the works of Thompson, Kitson and Richard Clutterbuck, is based on their experience of combating revolutionary war, insurgency and terrorism in their erstwhile colonies, and in Northern Ireland.

The US Army and Marine Corps Counterinsurgency Field Manual (2006) discuss "Historical Principles", "Contemporary Imperatives" and "Paradoxes of Counterinsurgency" under "aspects of counterinsurgency;" and outline "five over-arching requirements for successful counterinsurgency operations."

Indian Army doctrine is contained in its General Staff Publication "Special Operations—Part 8—Counter Insurgency Operations, 1990". It is further amplified in training memorandums issued by Army Headquarters; training notes issued by Headquarters Army Training Command; Precise issued by field formations. While the army's doctrine concentrates on the military aspects of counter-insurgency operations, it includes references to the role, responsibilities and functions of the government, the civil administration and the police forces. However, there is little to suggest that the civil government corroborates and endorses the army's view.

In the last decade, the army has published its doctrine for sub-conventional operations. It dwells on the "Various Prongs of the National Initiative"—"creation of secure environment"; "isolation of conflict zone"; and "public information and perception management". It also outlines a "Concept of Application of Military Force"—"people centric operations"; "maneuver versus attrition warfare"; "integrated approach"; "lines of military operations"; and "constitution of think tanks".

Despite differences of language and terminology, current British, US and Indian doctrines have much in common. All three acknowledge the long-term political nature of conflict; the imperatives of isolating the insurgent, mobilising the people, exercising restraint in the use of force, operating according to the law and achieving unity of effort; and the vital role of intelligence. However, with each country, there are variations in perception and emphasis.

The British accord importance to deciding on a political aim and a political programme. In the US doctrine the primary concern is to ensure effective governance by the host nation. India endorses the need to create a "favourable political climate". However, it pays insufficient attention to finding a political solution and "mobilising" the people in support of the government.

The US is "obsessed" with legitimacy of its own intervention and that of the host nation government. Britain is firm on the government "functioning in accordance with the law" but is unafraid to introduce emergency legislation. In India, the right of the union government to respond to internal threats to the security of the state is unquestioned, but it is reluctant to review, revise and change the ways in which domestic law is administered.

British doctrine is emphatic—a "government which ignores the international dimension of a counter-revolutionary campaign does so at its peril". Similarly, the US seeks international understanding and support for its interventions. India, on the other hand, avoids attracting outside attention to conflict within the state. It does not feel compelled to explain the "righteousness" of the government's cause in international circles, and yet, when faced with hostile interference by an external power, it seeks the understanding and support of the international community. Surprisingly, India completely overlooks the need to deny external support to insurgent movements within: the *bête noire* of counter-insurgency in India.

Despite the terms "unified command" and "joint civil-military responsibility" finding mention in Indian doctrine, the government fights shy of taking steps that will ensure "unity of effort".

Clearly, country-wise counter-insurgency doctrines are nuanced depending on whether operations have an "internal" bias within the homeland or "external" bias within the homeland of a host nation. No attempt is made to draw a distinction between the fundamental principles of counter-insurgency that are applicable to the government and the principles that are applicable to security forces (military) operations. As a consequence fundamental principles have a strong security-related flavour and lack accent on aspects of civil counter-insurgency.

8

Psychology and Terrorism

Dr. Sushama Bhosale

In modern times, terrorism is considered a major threat to society. Terrorism has surely existed since before the dawn of recorded history and human nature has not changed. However, three interlocking trends have significantly changed the nature and degree of the threat, i.e. the globalisation of commerce, travel, and information transfer, which puts economic disparities and ideological competition in sharp relief and facilitates cooperative aggression by far-flung but like-minded conspirators; the ascent of religious fundamentalism as an aggrieved competitor with the market-economic, democratic, and secular trends of modernity; and the privatisation of weapons of mass destruction, putting the potential of macro terrorist acts into the hands of small groups or even individuals (Hoffman 1998; Laqueur 1999; Enders and Sandler 2000). Terrorism is, in its broadest sense, the use of intentionally indiscriminate non peace action violence as a means to create terror or fear, in order to achieve a political, religious, or ideological aim. According to data from the Global Terrorism Database, more than 61,000 incidents of non-state terrorism, claiming over 140,000 lives, have been recorded from 2000 to 2014 (GTI, 2015). Terrorist activity increased by 80 percent in 2014 to its highest recorded level. The largest ever year-on-year increase in deaths from terrorism was recorded in 2014, rising from 18,111 in 2013 to 32,685 in 2014. The number of people who have died from terrorist activity has increased nine-fold since the year 2000. Boko Haram overtakes ISIL to become the most deadly terrorist group in the world. Deaths attributed to Boko Haram increased by 317 percent in 2014 to 6,644. ISIL was responsible for 6,073 terrorist deaths. Terrorist activity is highly concentrated—five countries accounted for 78 per cent of deaths. Fifty-seven per cent of all attacks and 78 percent of all deaths occurred in only five countries: Iraq, Nigeria, Afghanistan, Pakistan and Syria. Almost 60 percent of the countries covered in the GTI experienced no terrorist deaths in 2014. Ninety-five of the 162 countries covered in the study experienced no deaths from terrorism, while 67 countries experienced one or more deaths from terrorist activity. However, a majority of countries did experience a terrorist incident of some kind. Ninety-three countries experienced a terrorist incident in 2014, up from 88 in 2013. More countries than ever have high levels of terrorism. Countries suffering from more than 500 deaths were increased by 120 percent. In 2014, 11 countries had over 500 deaths while in 2013 only five did. Thirteen times as many people are killed globally by homicides than die in terrorist attacks. At least 437,000 people are victims of homicide each year, which is over 13 times more than the number of victims of terrorism (GTI 2015).

Correlates and Drives of Terrorist: Terrorist activity is correlated with political violence. The research found that 92 percent of all terrorist attacks between 1989 and 2014 occurred in countries where political violence by the government was widespread. Terrorism is also intrinsically linked to a country's safety and security environment. In the last 25 years, 88 percent of all terrorist attacks occurred in countries that were experiencing or involved in violent conflicts. Less than 0.6 per cent of all terrorist attacks occurred in countries without any ongoing conflict and any form of political terror. Lack of respect for human rights and for international organisations also correlates with terrorism. Other important correlates aside from political terror and ongoing conflict include lower respect for human rights, the existence of policies targeting religious freedoms, group grievances, political instability and lower respect for the UN or the EU. There are different drivers of terrorism in wealthier countries than in poorer countries. In OECD countries socio-economic factors such as youth unemployment, confidence in the press, faith in democracy, drug crime and attitudes towards immigration correlate significantly. In non-OECD countries factors such as a history of armed conflict, ongoing conflict within the country, corruption and a weak business environment are more strongly correlated.

Fig. 1: A Chart Plotted from the data in the GTD. A total of 157,520 incidents are plotted

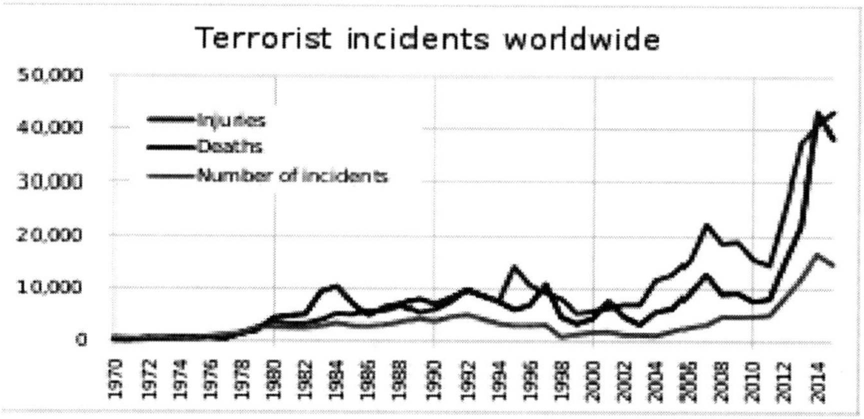

'Terrorism' comes from the French word '*terrorisme*', and originally referred specifically to state terrorism as practiced by the French government during the 1793–1794 Reign of Terror. The French word '*terrorisme*' in turn derives from the Latin verb '*terrere*' (e.g. terreo) meaning "to frighten". The Jacobins, coming to power in France in 1792, are said to have initiated the Reign of Terror (French: *La Terreur*). After the Jacobins lost power, the word 'terrorist' became a term of abuse. Although 'terrorism' originally referred to acts committed by a government, currently it usually refers to the killing of innocent people for political purposes in such a way as to create a spectacle. This meaning can be traced back to Sergey Nechayev, who described himself as a 'terrorist'. (GTI 2015).

Schmid (1983) compiled 109 academic definitions of terrorism, suggesting that there are roughly as many available definitions as there are published experts in the field. Nonetheless, two common elements are usually found in contemporary definitions: (1) that terrorism involves aggression against non-combatants, and (2) that the terrorist action in itself is not expected by its perpetrator to accomplish a political goal but instead to influence a target audience and change that audience's behaviour in a way that will serve the interests of the terrorist (Badey 1998) Laqueur 1999). The definition of terrorism has proven controversial. Various legal systems and government agencies use different definitions of terrorism in their national legislation. Moreover, the international community has been slow to formulate a universally agreed, legally binding definition of this crime. These difficulties arise from the fact that the term "terrorism" is politically and emotionally charged.

Table 1: Dimensions of Terrorism

Variable	*Classification*
Perpetrator number	Individual vs. group
Sponsorship	State vs. sub state vs. individual
Relation to authority	Anti-state/anti-establishment/separatist vs. pro-state/pro-establishment
Military status	Civilian vs. paramilitary or military
Financial motivation	Idealistic vs. entrepreneurial
Political ideology	Leftist/socialist vs. rightist/fascist vs. anarchist
Spiritual motivation	Secular vs. religious
Willingness to die	Suicidal vs. Non-suicidal
Target	Property (including data) vs. individuals vs. masses of people
Methodology	Bombing, assassination, kidnapping/hostage taking, mass poisoning,rape, other (e.g. bioterrorism, cyberterrorism)

The typology of terrorism is complex and controversial since actors can be characterised across multiple variables. Schultz (1980) proposed seven such variables might be specified for revolutionary versus sub-revolutionary terrorism. Post (2004) usefully divided political substate terrorism into: (1) social revolutionary terrorism, (2) right-wing terrorism, (3) nationalist-separatist terrorism, (4) religious extremist terrorism, and (5) single-issue (e.g. animal rights) terrorism, proposing that each type tends to be associated with its own social-psychological dynamics. A more comprehensive typology is shown in Table 1, listing variables subject to analysis and classifications within those variables.

Overview of Psychological Theories: Attempts to account for the behaviour of terrorists fall into two general categories: top-down approaches that seek the seeds of terrorism in political, social, economic, or even evolutionary circumstances and bottom-up approaches that explore the characteristics of individuals and groups that turn to terrorism (Wieviorka 1993, 2004).

How and Why Do People Enter and Stay in Terrorism?

Social and operational observations of numerous terrorist and extremist groups, however, suggest that recruitment and involvement in terrorism results from gradual exposure and socialisation towards extreme behaviour. Among the key psychological factors in understanding whether, how and which individuals in a given environment will enter the process of becoming a terrorist are motive and vulnerability. By definition, *motive* is an emotion, desire, physiological need, or similar impulse that acts as an incitement to action, and *vulnerability* refers to susceptibility or liability to succumb, as to persuasion or temptation. One's motivation for engaging in terrorism is often presumed to be the "cause" or ideology of the group. However, as Crenshaw (1985) notes, "the popular image of the terrorist as an individual motivate exclusively by deep and intransigent political commitment obscures a more complex reality." That reality is that motives to join a terrorist organisation and to engage in terrorism vary considerably across different types of groups, and also within groups – and they may change over time. The term "ideology" often carries a negative connotation. Ideology is often defined as a common and broadly agreed upon set of rules to which an individual subscribes which help to regulate and determine behaviour (Rokeach, 1979; Taylor, 1991). Aaron Beck (2002) recently applied a cognitive model to terrorist ideologies and concluded that, "The thinking of the terrorist evidently shows the same kind of cognitive distortions observed in others who engage in violent acts, either solely as individuals or as members of a group. These include over generalisation that is the supposed sins of the enemy may spread to encompass the entire population. Also, they show dichotomous thinking that a people are either totally good or totally bad. Finally, they demonstrate tunnel vision once they are engaged in their holy mission (e.g., jihad), their thinking, and consequently their actions, focuses exclusively on the destruction of the target." Based on examination of the existing professional literature and consideration of a variety of extremist ideologies, there are three general conditions that seem necessary for an ideology to support terrorism. First, the ideology must provide a set of beliefs that guide and justify a series of behavioural mandates. Bandura argues that, "People do not ordinarily engage in reprehensible conduct until they have justified to themselves the morality of their actions." Terrorists, like most others, seek to avoid internal conflict or dissonance by acting in ways that are consistent with their own beliefs and that allow them to see themselves as basically good. In essence, "Terrorists must develop justifications for their terrorist actions" (Cooper, 1977). Second, those beliefs must be inviolable and must be neither questionable nor questioned. Eric Hoffer pointed out the importance of belief for the human mind and the problems that arise when uncertainty in belief cannot be tolerated. Belief provides meaning and purpose-it reduces uncertainty and facilitates adaptation and adjustment. It offers "deep assurance" and "communion" with others. The beliefs on which the terrorist ideology is based cannot be doubted, criticised or skeptically examined. Indeed, among those who subscribe to the ideology, "to rely on the evidence of the senses and of reason is heresy and treason. It is startling to realise how much unbelief is necessary to make belief possible (Hoffer, 1951, p.83). Keane (2001) has similarly noted that, "For terrorism to succeed it demands firstly a rigid adherence to a simple idea. The mind that questions, debates and opens itself to challenging ideas, will prove a source of division for a terrorist movement in the heat of battle. Sticking to a rigid orthodoxy offers security and justification to people committing acts of terror." Third, the behaviours must be goal directed and seen as serving some meaningful cause or objective. People strive for meaning, and perhaps no cause has greater meaning than the polemic struggle between good and evil, in its various forms (McCormick, 2003). Evidence of this dynamic figures prominently into most terrorist ideologies. Falk (1988) even suggests that, "The terrorist mindset is dominated by its melodramatic preoccupation with the destruction of evil." Kernberg (2003) argues that such dichotomous, absolutist, "black and white" thinking ,especially concerning matters of morality, is a common feature of fundamentalist ideologies in general. He has observed that such ideologies, "divide the world into ideal and evil realms; their own ideology belongs to the ideal realm. The ideas beliefs and behavior of the realm of evil are immoral, dangerous, destructive, and threatening. Typically, such an ideology projects all aggression on to the evil social group, while justifying aggression against the infidel as a necessary defense and retribution if not a moral imperative" (Kernberg, 2003). Many analysts have commented on how this polarized moral polemic provides fertile ground for prescriptions of violence (Baumeister, 1997; Post, 1987; Schorkopf, 2003; White, 2001,). The role and influence of culture on terrorism generally and on terrorist ideologies specifically has been virtually neglected by most social science researchers. Brannan and colleagues have stated that there is one fundamental issue of culture relevant to such understanding that is rarely mentioned in terrorism studies and yet the virtual absence of which is an unambiguous sign of the flawed methodology currently in vogue (Brannan et.al., 2001, p. 14). Knutson (1981) observed from the life histories available for terrorists that these are acting upon values into which they have been comfortably socialised—both directly by teaching, and indirectly by life experiences of themselves and important others. However, these social-cultural political values which are sanguine to a revolutionary terrorist identity are a necessary but not sufficient ingredient in the formation of the terrorist.

Overview of Psychological Theories

Attempts to account psychological theories for the behaviour of terrorists fall into two general categories, top-down approaches that seek the seeds of terrorism in political, social, economic, or even evolutionary circumstances and bottom-up approaches that explore the characteristics of individuals and groups that turn to terrorism (Wieviorka 1993, 2004).

Fig. 2: Psychological Theories

Psychopathological	Social Learning	Psychoanalytic	Non-Psychoanalytic	Group Process
Rational Choice Theory	Frustration Aggression Theory	Identity Theory	Humiliation Revenge Theory	
Relative Deprivation	Narcissism Theory	Novelty Seeking Theory		
Oppression Theory			Cognitive Theories	
National Culture Theory				

I. Psychopathological Theory: Western psychiatry identifies adult behavioural disorders according to a multi-axial classification scheme in which Axis I refers to the major clinical illnesses—those such as schizophrenia or major depression—while Axis II refers to personality disorders—such as antisocial personality disorder (APD) (American Psychiatric Association 2000). APD is the current term for a pattern of remorseless disregard for the rights of others that was called *psychopathy* up until the mid-1950s and *sociopathy* thereafter. *Psychosis* refers to a loss of reality testing observed primarily in a subgroup of Axis I disorders (e.g. schizophrenia) but is *not* expected in Axis II disorders such as APD. *Insanity* is not a behavioural science term but a legal term that *usually* implies psychosis, although its definition is subject to significant jurisdictional variance (Resnick and Noffsinger 2004). Hence, a psychotic or "insane" person is so mentally disordered as to not know right from wrong, while a sociopath knows right from wrong and chooses wrong for selfish reasons without pangs of conscience. Terrorist groups are sometimes led by insane individuals, and while a few terrorist acts might be attributed to unequivocally insane persons, terrorists rarely meet psychiatric criteria for insanity. Rather, most of the literature attributing clinical mental disorder to terrorists speaks of the remorseless personality type, psychopathy or sociopathy (Taylor 1988). Pearce (1977) stated that terrorists were sociopaths acting antisocially due to "superego lacunae," meaning gaps in self-monitoring; he supports his conclusion such as the German student who joined the 1970s Red Army Faction or the Christian-to-Muslim convert who joins a modern radical Islamic cell, stand against their own and might be regarded as antisocial. Further evidence of the pro-sociality of some terrorists comes from the empirical work of Italian sociologist Donatella della Porta (1988) among 1,214 Italian militants, 351 (45.6 percent) enjoyed personal ties with eight or more group members before joining a terrorist organisation.

Rational Choice Theory: This theory explains that terrorist action derives from a conscious, rational, calculated decision to take this particular type of action as the optimum strategy to accomplish a sociopolitical goal (Crenshaw 1992; Wilson 2000). Rational choice theory, derived from economics, assumes this terrorist behavioural proclivity as a given and attempts to explain how changes in policy—the rules of the "game" that is played between terrorists and governments—might predictably alter behaviour. Since rational choice theory considers both policy and individual behavioural responses to policy, it combines the top-down and bottom-up approaches. Sandler and Arce (2003) listed six strengths of modern game theory for revealing quantifiable factors theoretically underlying the behaviour of terrorists and targeted governments: game theory: (1) captures the interdependent nature of such interactions; (2) helps discover the strategic implications when each side acts according to its best guess about how the other side thinks; (3) incorporates the impact of threats and promises from each side; (4) takes advantage of the observation that "players" tend to maximise goals subject to constraints; (5) helps predict outcomes in bargaining over demands; and (6) acknowledges the impact of uncertainty—incomplete information—on all the above. Strategic choice theory potentially offers vital insights into the potential payoff of terrorist versus government actions. Al Qaeda's brutal transnational campaign, including the mass murders at New York's World Trade Center in 2001, may have not only rapidly advanced Osama bin Laden's stated goal of removing the large U.S. military presence from Saudi Arabia but also served as an extremely potent recruiting tool (Whittaker 2001). Thus, historical precedents support many terrorists' expectations of success, so the theory of strategic choice must not be discounted on the grounds that terrorism's goals are uniformly improbable.

II. Social Learning Theories: Bandura's (1973, 1998) social learning theory of aggression suggests that violence follows observation and imitation of an aggressive model. Terrorist didactic learning also occurs via the dissemination of terrorist philosophy and methodology in communiqués, audiovisual tapes, compact disks, books, and Websites. Teenagers living in hotbeds of political strife may directly witness terrorist behaviours and seek to imitate them or, even more commonly, learn from their culture's public glorification of terrorists— for example, the "martyr posters" lining the streets of Shi'a regions of Lebanon and Palestinian refugee camps or the songs celebrating the exploits of the PIRA (Crenshaw 1992; Kelly and Rieber 1995). Social learning of the acceptability of terrorist violence may also take a didactic form, as in the teaching of an extremist form of jihad in many Pakistani and Palestinian *madrasas*—religious schools for young Muslim boys.

Frustration Aggression Theory: The basic premise of the frustration-aggression (FA) hypothesis is twofold: (1) Aggression is always produced by frustration, and (2) Frustration always produces aggression. Political psychologist John Chowing Davies (1973, 251) has even stated, "Violence is *always* a response to frustration". Though terrorist violence of either groups or individuals might be explained by this theory but it has been criticized on several grounds: millions of people live in frustrating circumstances but never turn to terrorism, many terrorists do not belong to the desperate classes whose frustration they claim to be expressing, and terrorism does not uniformly appear to be an act of last resort by those who have exhausted alternate approaches (Billig 1976; Merari and Friedland 1985; Sidanius and Pratto 1999).

Relative Deprivation Theory: Gurr's (1970) theory of relative deprivation proposed that economic disparities cause terrorism. This claim underlies— that rebellions come to be when people cannot bear the misery of their lot. There is a sociological link between poverty and terrorism (Krueger and Maleckova 2002). The major European revolutions of the eighteenth through the early twentieth century were probably provoked, at least in part, by class disparities.

Oppression Theory: Many scientists, from sociologists to revolutionaries, contend that oppression provokes political violence. Particularly in the case of nationalist-separatist or ethnic-sectarian terrorism (e.g. ETA, PIRA, Hamas), actors often cite the injustice of their treatment by governments that rob them of identity, dignity, security, and freedom as the motive for their joining a terrorist group (Crenshaw 1986; Taylor and Quayle 1994; Post, Sprinzak, and Denny 2003). Even if perceived oppression could be shown to breed terrorism, it would never be a sufficient explanation.

National Cultural Theory: Weinberg and Eubank (1994) proposed that terrorism expresses itself differently in "collectivist" versus "individualist" cultures. According to this theory, in collectivist cultures, a person's identity is primarily derived from the social system, dividing the world strictly according to in-groups and out-groups and linking their personal well-being to the well-being of their group, while in individualist cultures, identity is derived from personal goals. Weinberg and Eubank propose that collectivists would be more likely than individualists to carry out terrorist attacks on out-groups, including foreigners. They used psychological rankings of IBM corporate employees in forty nations on a scale of individualism/collectivism, reporting that U.S. citizens were the most individualistic (score 91), Israelis were in the middle (54), and Third World nations tended to be the most collectivist, such as Pakistan at 14 and Columbia at 13. Comparing these rankings with reports of terrorist activity from the "International Terrorism: Attributes of Terrorist Events 1968-1977" (ITERATE) database (Mickolus 1980), they claim that the data support their prediction that collectivists are more likely to attack foreigners, while individualists are more likely to attack co-nationals or members of other individualist cultures.

III. Psychoanalytic Psychological Theories: Sigmund Freud viewed aggression more generally as an innate and instinctual human trait, which most should outgrow in the normal course of human development. Freud's psychoanalytic theory stated that humans had the energy of life force (*eros*) and death force (*thanatos*) that sought internal balance. Violence was seen as the "displacement" of *thanatos* from self and onto others Psychoanalysis is based on the proposition that much of mental life is unconscious, that psychological development proceeds in stages based on infantile sexual fantasies, and that psychological distress derives from unresolved intra psychic conflict regarding those fantasies (Gabbard 2000). Psychoanalytic approaches to terrorist behaviour may be roughly divided according to their emphasis on identity theory, narcissism theory and absolutist thinking.

Identity Theory: This theory proposed that candidates for terrorism are young people lacking self-esteem who have strong or even desperate needs to consolidate their identities (Olsson, 1988). It was observed that those with identity confusion are perhaps tormented by a sense of isolation, conceivably engaging in terrorist violence as an adaptive response to the pain of anomie .Young people turning to political violence in a desperate search for identity may act alone (e.g. perhaps Charles Bishop, a fifteen-year-old who flew a small airplane into a bank in early 2002, leaving a suicide note declaring his allegiance with al Qaeda) (Rosenberg, Waddell, and Smalley 2002).

Narcissism Theory: The psychoanalytic concept of narcissism is a damaged sense of self. Self-psychology emphasises the needs that an infant has for caring responses to develop normally. Failure of maternal empathy leads to damage to the self-image—so called narcissistic injury—that arrests development in one of two ways: persistent infantile grandiose fantasies or failure to internalise the idealised image of the parent the possible linkage between narcissism and terrorism was first advanced by Morf (1970). He proposed that political experience, such as the humiliation of subordination, might produce an adult narcissistic injury that might reawaken the psychological trait of infantile narcissism. The result might be a pathological exaltation of self (the genesis of the leader), the abandonment of independence to merge with the archaic omnipotent figure (the genesis of the follower), or a combination of these impulses, as seen in the egotistical yearning for glory under the mask of selflessness. Potential support for the importance of narcissism comes from Gustave Morf's (1970) clinical examinations conducted with prisoners held as members of the Front for the Liberation of Quebec (FLQ). Morf reported that these individuals exhibited narcissistic traits, wishing to put themselves at the centre of the universe and to become terrorists.

IV. Non-Psychoanalytic Psychological Theories: It consists of various concepts as cognitions, humiliation and novelty seeking behaviour.

Humiliation Revenge Theory: Humiliation—and the consequent internal pressure for revenge—is another psychological factor that has been hypothesized to drive terrorist violence (Juergensmeyer 2000). Revenge for humiliation by an oppressor is, in fact, an ancient cultural tradition with direct links to the current violence in the Middle East. The concept that feelings of humiliation or being taken advantage of gives rise to a passion for revenge is very familiar in forensic psychiatry and criminology and probably contributes to many nonpolitical murders (Schlesinger 2000; Meloy 2001).

Novelty-Seeking Theory: Non-psychoanalytic psychological theories attribute terrorism to specific innate aspects of temperament developmental theories supports that youngsters with aggressive temperaments would be disproportionately attracted to terrorist organisations and sensation and novelty seeking, a *normative* feature of adolescent development probably tied to expected changes in neural activity may play a role in the natural history of terrorist involvement. (Dahl 2004).

Cognitive Theories: Cognitive capacity refers to mental functions such as memory, attention, concentration, language, and the so-called "executive" functions, including the capacity to learn and follow rules, to anticipate outcomes, to make sensible inferences, and to perform accurate risk-benefit calculations (Lezak 1995). Taylor and Quayle (1994) speculated that young people joining terrorist groups make a fundamental attribution error, a cognitive bias inaccurately attributing devious and evil motives to those they perceive as oppressors.

V. Theories of Group Process: Friedland (1992) postulated that terrorism is a group phenomenon and the result of an *interaction* between social processes and individual dispositions. However, he proposes three conditions under which individual proclivity to violence are relatively minor factor in the group's terrorist turning: (1) deprivation is intense, (2) the group has ideologized its discontent, and (3) the group is cohesive and clearly differentiated from the out-group. Membership in a terrorist organisation offers disciples a heady liquor of a well-defined personal role, a righteous purpose, the opportunity for revenge for perceived humiliations, and the lifting of constraints on the expression of otherwise prohibited behaviours—freeing the member from personal responsibility for attacks on out-groups. Group forces, including ideological indoctrination, repetitive training, and peer pressures, have been hypothesized to influence the group's violence, whether or not individual members were predisposed to such behaviour (Crenshaw 1992). This may occur because collective identity subsumes individual identity.

Limits to Psychological Research on Terrorism

Terrorism, like a shark attack, wields tremendous psychological impact. It is rare but awesome, deriving almost mystical significance by virtue of the suddenness, drama, and outrageousness of its violence. Multiple practical and theoretical impediments have delayed the scientific psychological study of terrorism. Most of the practical barriers are obvious that terrorism research may involve expensive and inconvenient travel to politically unstable regions, is potentially dangerous, and raises ethical issues that may challenge institutional review boards. Language barriers—including the lack of expert translations of high-quality psychological instruments—frustrate collection of data. Authorities may deny scholars the access to incarcerated terrorists because of security concerns and the perception that such assessments are not pertinent to counterterrorism. A theoretical issue is that it seriously limits the utility of interviews with specific terrorists or groups. Funding has long been a problem, with limited federal support. A cultural divide also separates psychologist from law enforcement, intelligence, and military personnel, counterterrorism forces occupy an adversarial position and must steel themselves against any sympathetic consideration of the terrorist's position.

Conclusion

Terrorist behaviour is probably *always* determined by a combination of innate factors, biological factors, early developmental factors, cognitive factors, temperament, environmental influences, and group dynamics. Terrorists are psychologically extremely heterogeneous. The current thrust of strategic choice studies focuses on predicting the behaviour of committed terrorists. For the purposes of long-term security policy formulation, an increased emphasis should be placed on early prevention, that is, on the analysis of the interaction between those psychological, cultural, economic, and political factors that influence uncommitted but impressionable young people to turn toward terrorism. Meaningful research is likely to be interdisciplinary, empirical, controlled, ethical, conducted across levels of analysis, and directed at root causes and modifiable risk factors along the entire chain of causality from historical forces to childhood influences to the moment of a terrorist act.

REFERENCES

American Psychiatric Association. (2000). *Diagnostic and statistical manual of mental disorders.* 4th ed., text revision. Washington, DC: American Psychiatric Association

Badey, T.J. (1998). Defining international terrorism: A pragmatic approach. *Terrorism and Political Violence,* 10:90–107.

Bandura, A. (1973). *Aggression: A social learning analysis.* New York: Prentice Hall.

Bandura, A. (1998). Mechanisms of moral disengagement. In *Origins of terrorism: Psychologies, ideologies, theologies, states of mind,* edited by W. Reich, 161–92. Washington, DC: Woodrow Wilson Center Press.

Baumeister, R.F. (1997). *Evil: Inside human violence and cruelty.* New York: W.H. Freeman

Beck, A.T. (2002). Prisoners of Hate. *Behavior Research and Therapy.* 40(3): 209–16.

Billig, M. (1976). *Social psychology and intergroup relations.* London: Academic Press.

Brannan, D.W., Esler, P.F., & Strindberg, N.T.A. (2001). Talking to "terrorists": Towards an independent analytical framework for the study of violent substate activism. *Studies in Conflict & Terrorism,* 24(1): 3–24.

Crenshaw, M. (1985). An organizational approach to the analysis of political terrorism. *Orbis,* 29(3): 465–89.

Crenshaw, M. (1986). The psychology of political terrorism. In *Political Psychology,* edited by M.G. Hermann. San Francisco: Jossey-Bass, pp. 379–413.

Crenshaw, & Martha (1992). *Terrorism in Context*, p. 77.

Crenshaw, M (1992). How terrorists think: What psychology can contribute to understanding terrorism. In *Terrorism: Roots, impact, responses*, edited by L. Howard. New York: Praeger.

Cooper, H.H.A. (1977). What is a terrorist: A psychological perspective. *Legal Medical Quarterly*, 1: 16–32.

dellaPorta, D. (1988). Recruitment processes in clandestine political organizations: Italian left-wing terrorism. *International Social Movement Research*, 1:155–69.

Enders,W., and T. Sandler. (2000). Is transnational terrorism becoming more threatening? time series investigation. *Journal of Conflict Resolution*, 44:307–32.

Falk, R. (1988). The terrorist mind-set: The moral universe of revolutionaries and functionaries. In *Revolutionaries and Functionaries: The dual face of terrorism*, edited by R. Falk. New York: E.P. Dutton.

Fortna, Virginia Page (20 May 2015). Outcomes. International *Organization*, 69 (3): 519–56.

Friedland, N. (1992). Becoming a terrorist: Social and individual antecedents. In *Terrorism: Roots, impact, responses*, edited by L. Howard. New York: Praeger

Gabbard, G.O. (2000). Psychoanalysis. In *Kaplan and Sadock's comprehensive textbook of psychiatry*, 7th ed., edited by B.J. Sadock and V.A. Sadock, 563–607. Philadelphia: Lippincott Williams & Wilkins

"Global Terrorism Index 2015" (PDF). Institute for Economics and Peace. p. 33.

Gurr, T. (1970). *Why Men Rebel*. Princeton, NJ: Princeton University Press.

Hoffman, B. (1998). *Inside Terrorism*. New York: Columbia University Press

Hoffer, E. (1951). *The True Believer*. New York: HarperCollins

Juergensmeyer, M. 2000. *Terror in the Mind of God*. Berkeley: University of California Press.

Kelly, R.J., and R.W. Rieber. 1995. Psychosocial impacts of terrorism and organized crime: The counter finality of the practi co-inert. *Journal of Social Distress and the Homeless*, 4:265–86.

Keane, F. (2001). The mind of a terrorist. J. Baxter, & M. Downing *The day that shook the world: Understanding Sept. 11* (pp. 54–67). London: BBC Worldwide.

Kernberg, O. F. (2003). Sanctioned Social Violence: A Psychoanalytic View - Part I. *International Journal of Psychoanalysis*, 84: 953–68.

Knuston, J. N. (1981). Social and psychodynamic pressure toward a negative identity: the case of an American revolutionary terrorist. In *Behavioral and Quantitative Perspectives on Terrorism*, edited by Y. Alexander, & J.M. Gleason (pp. 105–50). New York: Pergamon.

Krueger, A.B., and J. Maleckova. (2002). Education, poverty, political violence, and terrorism: Is there a connection? Working Paper No. w9074, National Bureau of Economic Research. Available at http://papers.nber.org/papers/w90747.

Laqueur, W. (1987). *The age of terrorism*. Boston: Little Brown.

Laqueur, W. (1999). *The new terrorism: Fanaticism and the arms of mass destruction*. New York: Oxford University Press.

Lezak, M.D. (1995). *Neuropsychological assessment*. 3rd ed. New York: Oxford University Press.

Marsella, A.J. (2003). Terrorism: Reflections on issues, concepts, and directions. In F.M. Moghaddam & A.J. Marsella (Eds.), *Understanding terrorism: Psychosocial roots, consequences, and interventions* (pp. 11-47). Washington, DC.

Moghaddam, F.M. and Marsella, A.J. (eds.). *Understanding Terrorism: Psychosocial Roots,*

Consequences, and Interventions. Washington, DC: American Psychological Association; pp. 11–48.

Merari, A., and N. Friedland. (1985). Social psychological aspects of political terrorism. *Applied Social Psychology Annual*, 6:185–205.

McCormick, G.H. (2003). Terrorist Decision Making. *Annual Review of Political Science*, 6:473–507.

Meloy, J.R. 2001. Communicated threats and violence toward public and private targets: Discerning differences among those who stalk and attack. *Journal of Forensic Sciences*, 46:1211–13.

Olsson, P.A. (1988). The terrorist and the terrorized: Some psychoanalytic consideration. *Journal of Psychohistory*, 16:47–60.

Pearce, K.I. (1977). Police Negotiations. *Canadian Psychiatric Association Journal* 22:171-4.

Post, J. M., and S. N. Gold. (2002). The psychology of the terrorist: An interview with Jerrold M. Post. *Journal of Trauma Practice*, 1:83-100.

Post, J.M. (1987b). "It's us against them": The group dynamics of political terrorism. *Terrorism*, 10, 23–35.

Post, J. M., E. Sprinzak, and L.M. Denny. (2003). The terrorists in their own words: Interviews with thirty-five incarcerated Middle Eastern terrorists. *Terrorism and Political Violence*, 15:171–84.

Post, J.M. (1990). Terrorist psycho-logic: terrorist behaviour as a product of psychological forces. In W. Reich (ed.) *Origins of terrorism: Psychologies, ideologies, theologies, states of mind* (pp. 25–40). New York: Cambridge University Press.

Resnick, P. J., and S. Noffsinger. (2004). Competency to stand trial and the insanity defense. In *The American Psychiatric Publishing textbook of forensic psychiatry*, edited by R.I. Simon and L.H. Gold. Washington, DC: American Psychiatric Publishing.

Rokeach, M. (1979). Understanding human values: Individual and societal. New York: Free Press.

Rosenberg, D., L. Waddell, and S. Smalley. (2002). A troubled teenager's tragic flight plan. *Newsweek*, January 21.

Sandler, T., and D.G. Arce. (2003). Terrorism and game theory. *Simulation & Gaming* 34:319–37.

Schmid, A. (1983). *Political terrorism: A research guide to the concepts, theories, databases and literature. With a bibliography by the author and a world directory of "terrorist" organizations by A. J. Jongman*. Amsterdam: North Holland.

Schultz, R. (1980). Conceptualizing political terrorism—A typology. In *International terrorism: Current research and future directions*, edited by A.D. Buckley and D.D. Olson, 9-15. Wayne, NJ: Avery.

Schorkopf, F. (2006). Behavioral and social science perspectives on political violence.

Sidanius, J., and F. Pratto. (1999). *Social dominance: An intergroup theory of social hierarchy and oppression*. Cambridge, UK: Cambridge University Press.

Taylor, M. (1991). *The fanatics: A behavioral approach to political violence*. London: Brassey's.

Taylor, M. (1988). *The terrorist*. London: Brassey's

Taylor, M., and E. Quayle. (1994). *Terrorist lives*. London: Brassey's

Weinberg, L., and W. L. Eubank (1994). Italian women terrorists. *Terrorism: An International Journal*, 9:241–62.

Wieviorka, M. (1993). *The making of terrorism*. Translated by D.G. White. Chicago: University of Chicago Press

Wieviorka, M. (2004). Preface. In *The making of terrorism*. Translated by D.G. White. Reprint, Chicago: University.

White, J. R. (2001). Political eschatology. *The American Behavioral Scientist*, 44(6): 937–56.

Wieviorka, M. (1993). *The making of terrorism*. Translated by D.G. White. Chicago: University of Chicago Press.

Wilson, M. A. (2000). Toward a model of terrorist behavior in hostage-taking incidents. *Journal of Conflict Resolution*, 44: 403–24.

Whittaker, D. J. (2001). *The terrorism reader*. London: Routledge Kegan Paul.

9

Terrorism and Counterterrorism

Air Marshal Bhushan Gokhale

"Nothing, nothing can justify Terrorism"

—Mahamood Darwish (Palestine poet)

Introduction

Peace and conflict is not something new to mankind. As a result, there have been over 4000 battles and wars, which find mention in recorded history. However, these conflicts have mainly been between countries or their alliances. These have caused many human casualties but restricted mainly to the fighting troops till the Second World War; wherein due to mass air raids and use of atomic weapons, the collateral damage included many civilian lives.

Terrorism on the other hand is often resorted to against innocent civilians. As per 'Statista', the statistics portal, since between 2006 and 2016, over 200,000 causalities have taken place worldwide.[1] It is a scourge impacting almost all the nations today and is considered a somewhat low-cost option to wage a proxy war against another country or support disgruntled groups of citizens within another country to take up armed violence.

India too has been affected by terrorism both sponsored from outside and also promoted internally. Very often strife in the Kashmir Valley sponsored mainly by Pakistan comes into focus, but of equal concern is the rapid spread of Naxal movement in last 25 odd years in regard to the country's internal security. While the Indian Army, Para-Military Forces and Police are employed in counterterrorist operations, in order to create shock and awe effect, the terrorist have often targeted innocent civilians. According to South Asia Terrorism Portal, there have been a total of 44171 casualties due to terrorism in India from 1988 till 12th February 2017. These include 14743 civilians, 6276 security personnel and 23152 terrorists.[2]

Genesis of Terrorism

The word *Terror* finds origin in Latin and 'terrere' in French, which means to frighten, and *Terrorism* refers to the systematic use of terror as a means of coercion. Although one finds usage of terror in mythology, its usage as a state policy in the form of 'Reign of Terror' was unleashed during the French Revolution. Intimidation and coercion to cause fear and panic amongst civilians thereby subjugating them into 'toeing the line' was the underlying principle. However, the reverse of this very application is now being used by various terrorist groups to propagate their beliefs or ideology in subjugating the State itself into acceding to their demands or else accept losing faith of the people who get intimidated by the terrorist acts of 'violent extremism'.

While there are different types of reasons or ideologies which are espoused by the terrorist groups, the means adopted have changed over the years. Hijacking of civil airliners, shooting of sports personnel like the Israeli football team in Berlin Olympics, blowing up hotels or embassies by planting bombs or by ramming aircraft themselves into buildings of the World Trade Centre as carried out on 11th September 2001 in New York. In recent years ISIS and Boko Haram in particular have not only kidnapped and killed innocent civilians but have resorted to videotaping the beheading and other violent acts to terrorise the people and governments.

India has also suffered all types of violence and various types of means used by terror groups in Kashmir, North East and the Maoists have a number of common methodologies. It is well known that a nexus of sorts exists between various terrorist organisations be it for funding, supply of arms and explosives as well as for training. In recent times LTTE had pioneered the concept of suicide bombing technique to enable undetected mingling within the crowds before blowing the human bomb. Such 'lone wolf' suicide attacks are expected to increase in future especially as the security forces are employing better counterterrorism techniques.

Definition of Terrorism

Terrorism is a global phenomenon which is affecting every continent. Although it is easy to recognise but the global bodies such as the UN have found it difficult to define. Experts and scholars from different countries tend to define it according to their socio-economic and political conditions. Countries affected by social and economic disparities view terrorism as a conflict in society between the haves and the have-nots. Naxalism can be considered in this category. On the other hand, those experiencing use of terror to gain more autonomy and self-governance like in Kashmir becomes a political phenomenon made complex when a neighbouring country, viz. Pakistan, aids such terrorist acts. As such the word 'terrorism' gets interpreted to suit different interests' groups.

Since there are innumerable definitions and interpretations of terrorism, multiple interpretations not only complicate the common response, but it also encourages its perpetrator to escape the gravity in the name of economic deprivation and freedom fighting. However, if these definitions are analysed in totality, an acceptable definition could be evolved. An American scholar, Brian Whitaker says that the definition preferred by the US State department is 'Premeditated, politically motivated violence perpetrated against non-combatant targets by sub-national groups or clandestine agents, usually intended to influence an audience.'[3] Further, 'International' terrorism is defined as 'terrorism involving citizens or the territory of more than one country'.[4] The key point about terrorism, on which almost everyone agrees, is that it is politically motivated. This is what distinguishes it from normal cases of murder or hooliganism.

Terrorism is often referred, though somewhat loosely, in many ways such as militancy, insurgency or an armed uprising. Scholars all over the world are entangled in the labyrinth of terminology and have expressed different views. Amongst them, the most widely acceptable definition is the one offered by Yonah Alexander. He defines terrorism as: 'the use of violence against random civilian targets in order to intimidate or to create generalised pervasive fear for the purpose of achieving political goals.'[5] While this definition is often quoted by experts, but it lacks an important aspect of terrorism, i.e. international linkages. Terrorists cannot inflict terror without the funds and infrastructure facilities that they receive from international connections.

Indian Definition of Terrorism

According to the Home Ministry, terrorism in India, poses a significant threat to the people of India. Terrorism in India includes ethno-nationalist terrorism, religious terrorism, left wing terrorism and narco-terrorism. The 8th report on terrorism in India published in 2008 defines terrorism 'as the peacetime equivalent of war crime'.[6] An act of terror in India includes any intentional act of violence that causes death, injury or property damage, induces fear, and is targeted against any group of people identified by their political, philosophical, ideological, racial, ethnic, and religious or any other nature. This description is similar to one provided by the United Nations in 2000.[7]

The Indian government uses the following working definition of terrorism, same as one widely used by Western nations as well as the United Nations, proposed by Alex Schmid and Albert Jongman in 1988[8]: 'Terrorism is an anxiety-inspiring method of repeated violent action, employed by (semi-) clandestine individual, group or state actors, for idiosyncratic, criminal or political reasons, whereby the direct targets of violence are not the main targets. The immediate human victims of violence are generally chosen randomly (targets of opportunity) or selectively (representative or symbolic targets) from a target population and serve as message generators. Threat and violence-based communication processes between terrorist organisation, victims, and main targets are used to manipulate the main target (audience(s)), turning it into a target of terror, a target of demands, or a target of attention, depending on whether intimidation, coercion, or propaganda is primarily sought.'

Definition of Terrorism in Pakistan and China

Created during the "Islamisation" of Pak Army in General Zia's presidency and used by the "deep state" as an undeclared policy to spread terror, Pakistan is now being devoured by the Frankenstein it has created. Pakistan calls these misguided holy warriors or Mujahideen, while the rest of the world calls these terrorists. During the Soviet-Afghan war, these fighters got trained and armed by Pakistan with assistance from the US, China, Saudi and many other countries then inimical to the Soviet Union. However, even after the withdrawal of Soviet troops from Afghanistan in 1979, the Mujahideen continued to form different groupings using terror as a weapon to destabilise not only the Af-Pak region but to assert radical Islamisation in rest of the world finally resulting into 9/11 and the resultant "War on Terror". Taliban, Al-Qaida and the ISIS have all been nurtured in some form or the other in Pakistan. Terror training camps in Pakistan have lured hundreds of youth into radical ideology and exported these armed terrorists all over the world including in Kashmir and Singkiang. The same groups are now taking on the state of Pakistan itself, making it the biggest threat to the citizens of Pakistan. Syed Manzar Abbas Zaidi of Pakistan Policy Research Institute laments that despite passage of Anti-Terrorism Act (ATA) in 1997 and creation of 54 Anti-Terrorism Courts (ATC), the conviction rate remains very low[9], thereby indicating that Pakistani government is not serious about controlling this scourge of their own creation.

Chinese on the other hand have articulated terrorism in their law though the definition not only includes "activity" but also "thought" and "speech". This has brought out strong reaction from Human Rights Watch but the Chinese are known to neglect such criticism. As per Zunyou Zhou, a Chinese Scholar residing in Germany, terrorism is generally defined in China by four key elements: violence, target, motivation and organisation[10]. First, terrorism requires violence as its objective element. Violence is usually a criminal offence of certain gravity. Of the four elements, violence is the least controversial. The second element of terrorism is the immediate target for the violence. Traditionally, immediate targets are limited to persons. More recently, however, the term has tended to be stretched to include objects. The U.S. definition uses the term "non-combatant targets," officially interpreted to include both civilians and military personnel not deployed in a war zone or a war-like setting. By comparison, the Chinese definition does not specify any immediate targets.

Thirdly, terrorism is traditionally defined as politically motivated violence and thus traditional definitions typically require a political motivation as their subjective element. The U.S. definition describes terrorism merely as "politically motivated violence," without expounding on the "motivation". By contrast, the Chinese definition requires a motivation that "generates social panic" or "influences national policy-making". Lastly, in the past, terrorism had to be committed by individuals at the behest of an organisational entity. More recently, so-called "lone wolves" without affiliation to any organisation have also launched destructive attacks and may even pose a greater threat than that represented by organised groups. In this context of all the definitions, the Chinese one is clearly the broadest. However, it is paradoxical that the Chinese continue to use UN veto to thwart Indian efforts to declare Pakistan based Azhar Masood the mastermind of 26/11 Mumbai attacks and leader of banned terrorist group Jaishe-e-Mohammad, in spite of all other members of Security Council including Saudi Arabia, agreeing to the Indian proposal. It seems that the Chinese are in turn trying to secure cooperation from the Pakistan-based terrorists for the safety of their ambitious China Pakistan Economic

Corridor (CPEC). However, they should not ignore the lessons of history as the same terrorism they are presently supporting will in the form of multi-headed hydra also hurt them in near future. There is no such entity as a "good terrorist" and a "bad terrorist".

Types of Terrorism

There are various ways of categorising terrorism. The Homeland Security Department of USA classifies terrorism in the following five categories:

- **State-Sponsored terrorism:** This consists of terrorist acts on a state or government by a state or government.
- **Dissent terrorism:** These are terrorist groups that have rebelled against their government.
- **Terrorists and the Left and Right:** These are groups rooted in political ideology.
- **Religious terrorism:** These are terrorist groups that are extremely religiously motivated, and
- **Criminal terrorism:** These are terrorists acts used to aid in crime and criminal profit.

In India, as mentioned earlier, the 8th report on terrorism in India published in 2008 defines terrorism as the peacetime equivalent of war crime. An act of terror in India includes any intentional act of violence that causes death, injury or property damage, induces fear, and is targeted against any group of people identified by their political, philosophical, ideological, racial, ethnic, and religious or any other nature. As such, India subdivides terrorism in four major groups:

Ethno-nationalist Terrorism: This form of terror focuses either (a) on creating a separate State within India or independent of India or in a neighbouring country, or (b) on emphasising the views/response of one ethnic group against another.

Religious Terrorism: This form of terror focuses on religious imperatives, a presumed duty or in solidarity for a specific religious group, against one or more religious groups. Mumbai 26/11 terror attack in 2008 from an Islamic group like JeM in Pakistan is an example of religious terrorism in India.

Left-wing Terrorism: This form of terror focuses on economic ideology, where all the existing socio-political structures are seen to be economically exploitative in character and a revolutionary change through violent means is essential. The ideology of Marx, Engel, Mao, Lenin and others are considered as the only valid economic path. Maoist violence in many states of India, including Jharkhand and Chhattisgarh, are examples of left-wing terrorism in India.

Narco-Terrorism: This form of terror focuses on creating illegal narcotics traffic zones. Drug money gets invariably used to fund terror groups. ISI of Pakistan has been using such funds to train and equip radicalised youth.

In addition to above types Cyber-terrorism is increasingly gaining importance as the network hacking can cause havoc in various fields of banking, tele-communications, and even for control of strategic weapons. Similarly uses of radiation material or biological agents to spread harmful agents are the newer threats, as the terrorists get more tech savvy. Eco-terrorism relates to intentional sabotage of the environment, water sources and other natural resources.

It is worth noting that as per the South Asian Terror Portal, as many as 180 plus terrorist groups have operated within India over the last 20 years[11], many of them co-listed as transnational terror networks operating in or from neighbouring South Asian countries. Out of these approximately 40 are on the current list of terrorist organisations banned by India and many of these including JeM are also banned by the US, EU and the world bodies.

Counter Terrorism

Counter-Terrorism includes measures adopted by the security agencies to prevent terrorism. These measures include overall strategy of the government, tactics and techniques which are adopted by the military and other law enforcement agencies as well as those by the intelligence agencies. Since a lot of funding is required to train and equip the terrorists, counter-terrorism strategies include methods to detect and counter-financing of terrorism.

On 8th September 2006 the United Nations General Assembly has adopted the Global Counter-Terrorism Strategy, which is a unique global instrument to enhance national, regional and international efforts to counter terrorism. Through its adoption that all Member States have agreed the first time to a common strategic and operational approach to fight terrorism, not only sends a clear message that terrorism is unacceptable in all its forms and manifestation but also resolves to take practical steps individually and collectively to prevent and combat it. It is reviewed every 2 years and 2016 marks the 10th anniversary of the UN Global Counter-Terrorism Strategy. The strategy is based on 4 pillars of action to address the issue of terrorism comprehensively. These pillars include:

- Address the conditions conducive to the spread of terrorism.
- Measures to prevent and combat terrorism.
- Measures to build states' capacity to prevent and combat terrorism and to strengthen the role of the United Nations system in that regard.
- Measures to ensure respect for human rights for all and the rule of law as the fundamental basis for the fight against terrorism.

Unfortunately, in the fog of real-politic, the UN has not been able to take any firm action so far. Some of the UN Peace Keeping troops have also failed to implement suitable measures due to lack of consensus amongst the member states and the big powers.

In India, over the years a number of measures have been institutionalised to deal with militancy, insurgency and terrorism. With experience gained in Kashmir, Punjab, the North East and the Maoists, the government has been creating specially trained security forces like the Para Commandos, Ghatak, Marcos, Garud, Cobra, etc., to name a few. Similarly monitoring agencies like Multi Agency Centres to coordinate inputs from various intelligence agencies with the help of National Intelligence Grid (NATGRID) have been established. However, considering the federal structure of the country a centralised response centre or National Counter Terrorism Centre (NCTC) on the lines of USA has not been established yet. This needs to be hastened to create further synergy in intelligence gathering and sharing it rapidly where it is needed urgently. It is suggested by many experts that by establishing a Counterterrorism institute, the synergy will be enhanced further.

In dealing with terrorism the government has also tried to use a mix of hard and soft responses. Good governance and winning "hearts and minds" is of great importance in ensuring local support, though such efforts are often frustrated by external interference especially sponsored by Pakistan. The recent "surgical strike" of September 2016 has helped in indicating a firm political resolve apart from proving the capability of Special Forces.

Recommendations

Actionable Intelligence. Acquiring actionable intelligence by the security agencies in order to prevent a terrorist act is an extremely important starting point. While modern technology enables fair amount of monitoring, sifting through the large volume of metadata is very challenging. The intelligence agencies need different types of inputs, such as electronic, imaging, etc., but one of the most important inputs is always the human intelligence, which can be corroborative. Lack of human intelligence has been a bane for India for many years now. With over 12 different agencies engaged in accessing inputs, inter-agency coordination and passing of actionable information has been a problem. Though after the formation of Multi Agency Centre and NATGRID, there is far greater efficiency in recent times.

Intrusive Techniques and Loss of Personal Freedom. In order to distil various inputs, the intelligence agencies need to use intrusive techniques such as tapping phones, eavesdropping and scanning e-mails, etc. Invariably such actions are criticised by Human Rights agencies since there is a certain loss of personal freedom. However, the authorisation procedures as well as the legal provisions cater to certain precautions.

Global Co-operation. Since terrorism is now a global phenomenon with funding being done by many agencies under the garb of welfare schemes as also smuggling of explosives by covert means, there is a growing need for International cooperation to warn and thwart the impending terror attacks. India has been at the forefront in cooperating with Interpol or other country specific agencies.

Insider attack and Police verification. In a number of recent terrorist attacks, it has come to light that the infiltrators were invariably assisted by local contacts. This was reported during investigation into 26/11 and in Pathankot airfield attack. Unfortunately, lure of money or other reasons have entrapped Indian nationals and hence they have been facilitating terror attacks or have become "home-grown terrorists." There is a need to strengthen Police verification process of personnel engaged in working particularly at Military installations and also Counter Intelligence expertise for keeping such elements under watch need strengthening.

Role of Media in Glorifying the Act. It is well known that the terrorists bask in the glare of media. More the publicity they get, it adds to their propaganda and helps instilling fear amongst people. Hence, media needs to ensure unbiased reporting and only share credible news so that unfounded statements leading to rumours are avoided. We have come a long way from reporting live encounters of Mumbai 26/11 but even the "deferred telecast" can provide clues to the terrorist by their handlers especially in a protracted encounter.

Use of Social Media. Social media has been able to reach the masses overcoming limitations of geographical or electronic boundaries. In turn by means of using "Photoshop" or other softwares not only can the terrorist glorify their cause and effect but also use it in actual terror attack to instruct other members of their team. While some countries in the Gulf or China have tried to ban social media, electronic black-out or jamming networks are some of the techniques being used by the Indian Security agencies. These efforts need further strengthening.

Declaring Pakistan a "Terrorist State". While India has always dreamt of a stable and prosperous neighbourhood, Pakistan's active role in sponsoring terrorism in India is well known. India has even granted the status of Most Favoured Nation (MFN) to Pakistan. However, the "deep state" continues to use the policy of "bleeding India with thousand cuts". Recently President Trump of USA has banned entries to nationals from 6 Islamic countries. It is given to understand that Pakistan is also on the "watch" for their housing of terror camps which have not only affected India but also the US and other countries. Mounting pressure on Pakistan in the backdrop of the Uri terror attacks, two influential US Congressmen for the first time ever have introduced a legislation to designate Pakistan as a terror state. In this context it is noteworthy that without waiting for other countries to do so, Shri Rajeev Chandrasekhar, an Independent member of the Rajya Sabha had moved a bill on 24th September 2016 calling for India herself to declare Pakistan a "Terrorist State". Unfortunately, the passage of this bill is in doubt.

Conclusion

The menace of terrorism needs to be tackled firmly. While Pakistan continues to ferment trouble by sponsoring terror outfits it is unfortunate that China keeps supporting her proxy. While these aspects will continue to be in the realm of international politics India needs to strengthen her counterterrorism apparatus. On the other hand continued economic progress to allow education, employment and better living standards will ensure that the youth do not get lured into anti-national activities.

In the end it will be apt to quote some of the excerpts from the letter which Prime Minister Shri Narendra Modi wrote to the heads of 193 member-states of the United Nations on the occasion of its 70th Anniversary in October 2015.

"The United Nations must be made more effective for dealing with the new security challenges. The United Nations was born out of the ashes of the Second World War, when conflict was an inter-state phenomenon. However, we are now living in an era when non-state actors are a major factor. Terrorism and violent, intolerant extremism did not exist earlier as a primary threat to the nations and societies at large. Indeed, with expanded geographical spread, vast resources and new instruments to spread its ideology and draw recruits; the menace of terrorism and extremism has acquired a new dimension that requires a comprehensive global strategy. We must use this historic year to send an unambiguous message of zero tolerance against terrorism. An important step in this direction would be adopting the Comprehensive Convention against International Terrorism at the United Nations this year."

In my opinion, with synergy amongst the security forces, intelligence agencies, good governance, public co-operation and political resolve, it is possible to tackle the growing menace of terrorism.

Jai Hind!

NOTES

1 Statista. Number of casualties due to terrorism worldwide between 2006 and 2016. Statista. https://www.statista.com/statistics/202871/number-of-fatalities-by-terrorist-attacks-worldwide/

2 South Asia Terrorism Portal. http://www.satp.org

3 Whitaker, Brian (2001). The definition of terrorism. The Guardian. https://www.theguardian.com/world/2001/may/07/terrorism

4 US Dept. of State. LEGISLATIVE REQUIREMENTS AND KEY TERMS. https://www.state.gov/documents/organization/65464.pdf

5 Lazreg, Houssem Ben (2017). The debate over what constitutes terrorism. The Conversation. http://theconversation.com/the-debate-over-what-constitutes-terrorism-86812

6 Second Administrative Reforms Commission, GoI. Combatting Terrorism – Protecting by Righteousness. Eighth Report. https://darpg.gov.in/sites/default/files/combating_terrorism8.pdf

7 Terrorism. UN. https://www.un.org/News/dh/infocus/terrorism/sg%20high-level%20panel%20report-terrorism.htm

8 Schmid, Alex, &Jongman, Albert (1988). Political Terrorism: A New Guide to Actors,

Authors, Concepts, Data Bases, Theories, and Literature. https://books.google.co.in/books/about/Political_Terrorism.html?id=NgDks1hUjhMC&redir_esc=y

9 Zaidi, Syed Manzar Abbas (2016). Terrorism Prosecution in Pakistan. United States Institute of Peace. https://www.usip.org/publications/2016/04/terrorism-prosecution-pakistan

10 Zhou, Zunyou (2015). How China Defines Terrorism. The Diplomat. https://thediplomat.com/2015/02/how-china-defines-terrorism/

11 South Asia Terrorism Portal. India—Terrorist, insurgent and extremist groups. http://www.satp.org/terrorist-groups/india

10

Nuclear Terrorism: Investigating the Threat and Exploring Possible Scenarios

Arun Vishwanathan[1]

Introduction

Over the past couple of decades, we have been witness to terrorist groups increasingly adopting innovative methods and techniques. Innovation has been seen in the methods they employ for carrying out attacks, like use of drive by shootings, vehicle or human improvised explosive devices (IEDs), simultaneous attacks on multiple locations in urban spaces. While the use of such techniques has caused significant loss of life, injuries, damage to property, the use of such methods has also introduced an element of surprise, thereby making it difficult for the security forces to prepare for any such eventuality.

The second and equally worrisome trend has been greater use of technology by terrorist groups to recruit, train, plan and carry out terror attacks. The use of internet-based technologies, like social media, i.e. Twitter, Telegram, internet-based chat rooms, propaganda websites give the terrorist groups wider access to a larger pool of recruits cutting across national boundaries.[2] In the 2008 Mumbai terror attacks by the Pak-based terrorist group *Lashkar-e-Toiba* (LeT), we witnessed, inter alia, use of GPS devices to navigate to the landing locations by sea and pinpoint attack locations in the city. LeT has also employed Voice over Internet Protocol (VoIP) telephones to communications between the terrorist and their Pakistan-based handlers.

In addition to greater use of technology and innovativeness to carry out attacks by terrorist groups; we have also seen continuing efforts by terror groups, like the *Al Qaeda*, to acquire Weapons of Mass Destruction (WMD) that includes Nuclear, Biological and Chemical weapons. Rolf Mowatt-Larsenn has put together a chronology of Al Qaeda's efforts to acquire WMD, wherein the group has been making consistent efforts since 1993 to get access to uranium. The first of many such efforts was based in Sudan where the group attempted to acquire Uranium for a sum of US$1.5 million with the involvement of former Sudanese President, Saleh Mobruk.[3] These efforts, Rolf Mowatt-Larsenn claims, assumed greater "systematic, programmatic efforts" in 1998 after the merger of Ayman al Zawahiri's Egyptian Islamic Jihad with the Al Qaeda.[4]

Given the fact that acquiring WMDs and in particular nuclear weapons is an avowed goal of a major terrorist group like the Al Qaeda, it becomes important to pay due attention to ensuring security of fissile material and safety of nuclear power plants and other associated facilities. In order to perform this task efficiently and effectively, it is important to be able to distinguish between hyped and real threats.[5] This is where the nomenclature of "nuclear terrorism" itself becomes a hindrance. With the word nuclear attached to terrorism, every incident whether real, misreported or just pure rumour mongering becomes a priority thereby taking away precious time and resources away from attending to the real threats.

In 1995, the International Atomic Energy Agency (IAEA) put in place the IAEA Incident and Trafficking Database (ITDB) system. The system was strengthened after the September 2001 attacks. The 2016 factsheet put out by the ITDB mentions that 131 states participated in the ITDB programme.[6] The ITDB 2016 Factsheet states that there have been a total of 21 attempts to smuggle and sell weapons-usable fissile material between 1995 and 2015. Of these, 13 were confirmed incidents of unauthorised possession of highly enriched uranium, 3 incidents of unauthorised possession of plutonium and 5 cases of plutonium beryllium neutron being seized in unauthorised possession. Further, the report states that some of these incidents involved smuggling of the material across international borders for illegal sale. As Table 1 below highlights, IAEA statistics themselves establish the fact that in many cases, kilogram quantities of the weapons-usable nuclear material have been seized from black marketers and smugglers.[7]

Table 1: Incidents of unauthorised possession of >1 kg of HEU/Pu (1993-2004)[8]

Date	*Location*	*Material Involved*	*Incident Description*
March 1994	St. Petersburg, Russian Federation	HEU 2.972 kg	An individual was arrested in possession of HEU, which he had previously stolen from a nuclear facility. The material was intended for illegal sale.
December 1994	Prague, Czech Republic	HEU 2.73 kg	HEU was seized by police in Prague. The material was intended for illegal sale.
June 1995	Moscow, Russian Federation	HEU 1.7 kg	An individual was arrested in possession of HEU, which he had previously stolen from a nuclear facility. The material was intended for illegal sale.

What Makes the Risk of Nuclear Terrorism Real?

As the preceding paragraphs clearly establishes the fact that terrorist groups like the Al Qaeda have the intent and motivation to use WMDs including nuclear weapons. Terror groups have increasingly made greater use of technology and have shown a heightened level of technical awareness. Given the above, it is not beyond the realm of the probable, that in case they are able to secure access to sizeable quantities of weapon-usable fissile material they could use it to carry out acts of nuclear terrorism.

The risk of terrorist groups getting access to fissile material has been increasing in recent years due to three reasons. First, is the continued existence of large stockpiles of weapons-usable fissile material across the globe. Secondly, the expansion of civilian nuclear power programs and increasing number of nuclear power plants and associated facilities across the globe. The third reason that heightens the risk is the fact that terrorism and violent extremism has itself been growing across the globe.[9]

Expanding Nuclear Stockpiles

The 2015 Global Fissile Material Report released by the International Panel on Fissile Material (IPFM) has estimated the civilian and military stockpile of highly enriched uranium and plutonium fissile material across the globe.

Highly Enriched Uranium (HEU): All the Nuclear Weapon States as defined in the NPT, namely, China, France, Russian Federation, United Kingdom and United States have ceased production of HEU for weapons purposes. They, however, continue to produce HEU for fuelling their naval, submarine reactors. The IPFM 2015 report estimates that HEU stocks globally are 1370

±125 tons.[10] Assuming about 25kgs of HEU for simple first generation fission-based nuclear weapon, the stockpile will be enough for over 54,000 nuclear weapons.

Plutonium: The 2015 IPFM report estimates that the global stockpile of separated Plutonium (Pu) is about 505 ±10 tons of which about 234 tons was Pu for weapons use and 271 tons produced for civilian use. Assuming about 3kgs of weapons-grade plutonium/weapon, 234 tons of Pu fissile material translates into 70,760 weapons amount worth of material. Similarly, assuming that 5kg of reactor-grade Pu can be used to make a nuclear weapon, 271 tons Pu for civilian use can be used to manufacture 49,169 nuclear weapons.

The point in providing the above statistics is to share the amount of fissile material that has been accumulated by the nuclear-armed states, in particular the United States and the Russian Federation. Nuclear security, given the nature of the material, and the secretiveness of the institutions involved are inherently complex affairs. Ensuring foolproof security for such a large mass of fissile material across the globe is a time and resource consuming affair.

Expanding Nuclear Power Plants and Facilities

While nuclear power has been on the decline in the Western countries, since 2001, nuclear energy has witnessed a renaissance of sorts in Eastern Europe and Asia. A new spate of expansion of nuclear energy has been witnessed in these regions driven by increasing domestic energy demands, attempts to mitigate climate change concerns, address energy security concerns like disruption or rise in prices of conventional sources of energy like oil and gas.

The International Atomic Energy Agency's Power Reactor Information System (PRIS) states that currently there are 449 reactors under operation and 60 reactors under construction. An analysis of the statistics available in the PRIS highlights the fact that on an average 8 reactors started construction between the years 2008-16.[11] China with 20 reactors under construction far outstrips Russia and India; the next two countries in the list have 7 and 5 reactors that are currently under construction. See Figure 1 for a detailed breakup of the reactors currently under construction.

Fig. 1: Reactors under Construction Worldwide

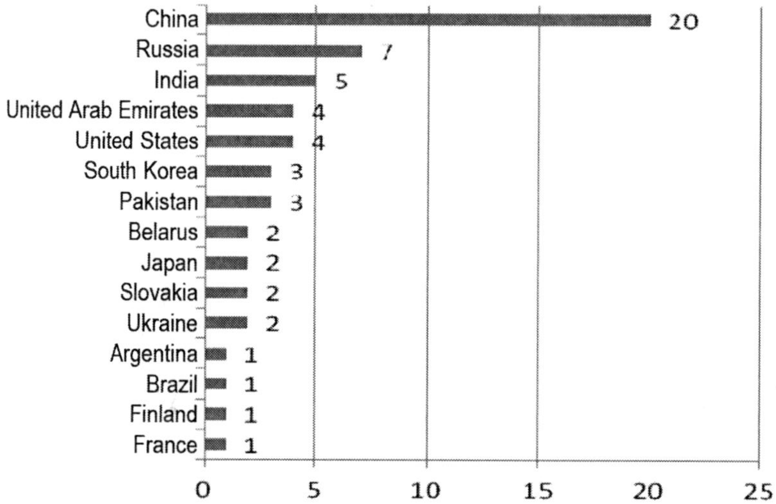

Current Approach to Nuclear Security

More often than not, the West has been prone to lecturing the rest of the world about nuclear security issues. Such an approach stems out of the false perception that nuclear weapons, material and facilities are safer in the West. The fact of the matter is that nuclear weapons are dangerous weapons and securing them, wherever that might be, is a complex affair. Take the example of what transpired on July 28, 2012, at the US's Y-12 weapons-grade uranium storage facility at Oak Ridge, Tennessee. The facility is a Category-1 facility where a large part of American weapon-grade highly enriched uranium (HEU) is stored in the HEU Materials Facility which stores about 449 tons of Highly enriched Uranium.[13]

Three unarmed senior citizens, which included an eight-two year old nun who were part of the Ploughshares movement and were protesting against nuclear weapons, managed to cut across four perimeter fences and were able to roam around freely in the facility for almost 90 minutes without being challenged within the Protected Area which is at the heart and is the most heavily guarded portion of the Y-12 facility. The reason behind why the trio was able to successfully circumvent many of the perimeter security alarms on the perimeter and reach the main building is a complex one. However, here it will suffice to say that the facility building was guarded by sensors and alarms which were prone to giving many false alarms. The guards at the facility had thus stopped answering the alarms and as a result failed to respond to the three Ploughshares activists breaking into the facility.[14]

The fact of the matter is that the above act of breaking into the Y-12 facility is not an isolated incident. Ploughshare activists have carried out similar actions across the United States. In the past, they have managed to get unauthorised access to the Kitsap Naval Base, which is the home port for more than half of America's Trident ballistic-missile submarines; the Andrews Air Force Base which stations the B-52 bombers; a Minuteman missile complex in eastern Colorado among other sites.[15]

The scary part of the above actions is the fact that it is possible for dedicated Ploughshares activists—with access only to public documents and maps and a year of planning—to break into the heavily guarded Y-12 facility with such ease. Terror groups, who are equally if not more motivated with access to the same information and with insider assistance could do better.

The above discussion points to need for world leaders to understand that there should be another way the issue should be approached. As Charles Perrow writes in the *Bulletin of Atomic Scientists*, "Our current approach to risk is 'probabilistic' …but we should also consider a worst case approach to risk, the 'possibilistic' approach." Simply put, currently countries are always preparing on the basis of the last attack but are generally ill-prepared for the attack that has never happened before.[16]

P.R. Chari writing for the Carnegie Endowment for International Peace highlights the issue of transparency which often comes up in many articles dealing with the issue of nuclear security.[17] Transparency is somehow seen as a panacea for all problems dealing with nuclear security, as if countries were to be more transparent all their issues surrounding nuclear security would be solved. The reverse has also been argued in the case of India. Just because of a lack of transparency, it has been stated that all is not well in India among other countries.[18] Though increased transparency and better communication would help in building trust and is important during crises, it is important to realise that given the catastrophic nature of events in case of a successful attack, governments cannot be completely transparent or free in sharing their plans beyond a point.

Thus, the problem we face is a complex one. On one hand, we are witness to the rise of terrorism as seen by the rise of the Islamic State in West Asia. Closer home, we are seeing regular terror attacks by Sunni terror groups in Pakistan. Also, these groups are becoming much more lethal and innovative and equally adept at using technology for recruitment, training and carrying out terror attacks. This problem gets compounded by the twin fact that large amounts of fissile material enough for making thousands of nuclear weapons is stored in isolated facilities located across the globe. For historical, economic and for pure logistical reasons, it is hardly possible to guard all these facilities and missile and weapon storage sites against all current and future attacks.

Nuclear Terrorism: Possible Scenarios

In order to prepare for as many eventualities as possible, it is necessary to outline the possible scenarios in which an act of nuclear terrorism could take place.

Explosion of a Nuclear Device: The worst possible situation would be the actual explosion of a nuclear device. This could take place if the terrorist is able to get access to fissile material and put together a working nuclear device. The other scenario could be detonation of a nuclear device in storage. In both these situations, the damage potential as well as the difficulty potential is "High" due to the lack of easy access to weapons storage or fissile material storage facilities. Insider assistance remains crucial whether to get access or in form of technical assistance to put together fissile material into a working nuclear weapon.

Sabotage of a Nuclear Power Reactor: The second possible scenario could be the sabotage of a nuclear power reactor or any other operational nuclear facility like a uranium enrichment facility or nuclear reprocessing plant. The aim of the terrorist in such an attack would be to override the existing safety controls in the facility and ensure atmospheric release of radioactivity. The damage potential and the difficulty of a successful operation is High. This is primarily because of the necessity of possessing technical expertise to override the safety features in place in such a facility, which would prevent radioactive release. Again, inside access and technical assistance would be crucial for the success of the endeavour. Given the fact that a nuclear power plant contains tons of nuclear fissile material, the damage potential in case of success of a terrorist attack would also be exponentially higher. As compared to the 64 kg of HEU in Little Boy, the bomb dropped on Hiroshima, the amount of fissile material in the Fukushima reactors at the time of the accident was 1852 tons. In terms of radioactivity released, the Little Boy released 89 Tera Becquerel of Cs-137 as compared to 15,000 terabecquerels of Cs-137 released following the Fukushima accident.[19]

Terrorist Attack on a Nuclear Storage Facility: The main aim of such an attack would be to get access to fissile material or detonating the facility with an aim of dispersing radioactivity/fissile material. As seen from the various successful attempts by Ploughshares activists, a lot of information about the location and the facilities is available in the public and more details could be gathered with minimal surveillance. Also, the complex nature of security and routine nature of the duties at these facilities causes fatigue amongst the employees which leads to laxity in implementing security controls as they are seen as cumbersome and time consuming. While insider assistance would be useful, it is not critical in planning and carrying out such an attack.

In the recent past, we have seen terrorist attacks taking place close to locations where nuclear missile storage facilities are stored in Pakistan. Shaun Gregory writing in the American West Point, Counter Terrorism Center Journal CTC Sentinel[20] highlights three such incidents:

- November 1, 2007—Attack on the nuclear missile storage facility at Sargodha
- December 10, 2007—Attack on Pakistan's nuclear airbase at Kamra by a suicide bomber
- August 21, 2008—Attack by Pakistani Taliban suicide bombers where several entry points to one of the armament complexes at the Wah cantonment were blown up. Wah cantonment centres are considered to be one of the facilities where Pakistan's main nuclear weapons are assembled.

Radiological Dispersal Device (RDD): RDD is essentially dispersal of radioactive material by detonating it with a high explosive. It is not very difficult for a terrorist group to carry out such an attack. Many radioactive isotopes are used in hospitals and laboratories. It is therefore quite easy for any such group to get access to these materials. However, an RDD is not a nuclear weapon as it would not create a chain reaction. The physical damage would be limited to injuries or deaths from the blast. However, a lot of panic would be created and the RDD would have to be followed up with an expensive clean-up operation which would hurt the economy and the public sentiment at large.

Table 2: Possible Types of Nuclear Terrorism Attacks and their Damage Potential and Difficulty Factor

Type of Nuclear Terrorism	*Damage Potential*	*Difficulty Factor*	*Reasons for difficulty*	*Dangers to beguarded against*
Nuclear Device Exploded	High	High	- Difficulty to get access to Fissile Material/ Weapon - Lack of Technical Expertise to put together the fissile material into a working nuclear weapon - Difficulty to override the PAL or other similar controls to prevent unauthorised use of nuclear devices.	- Nuclear Security at nuclear installations, missile storage and weapons storage sites need to be upgraded. - Insider Assistance very important.
Sabotaging a Nuclear Power Reactor	High	High	- Lack of Technical Expertise to cause a critical disruption by overriding safety checks which leads to release of radioactivity	- Gaining Access to the control room which is highly guarded. - Cyber Attacks - Insider Assistance very important
Terrorist Attack on a Nuclear Storage Facility with an aim to get access to fissile material or detonating the facility with an aim of dispersing radioactivity/fissile material	Medium to Low	Medium	- Difficulty to get access to the facility where the fissile material is stored.	- Given access to public information and maps, motivated groups have been able to get unauthorised access to these facilities. - Complex nature of security and routine nature of the duties causes fatigue amongst the employees. - Insider Assistance Useful
Radiological Dispersal Device (RDD)	Low	Low	- It is fairly easy to procure fissile material from hospital and laboratories. - dispersal of radioactive material by detonation with high explosive not very difficult for a terrorist group. - would not create a chain reaction - physical damage limited to explosive blast damage	- Controls, proper material accountancy and disposal of fissile material at hospital, laboratories.

Conclusion

As terrorist groups continue to adopt innovative means of carrying out attacks and make growing use of technology in such attacks, it becomes imperative to employ a "systems-approach" to security to prevent nuclear material and technology from landing in the hands of terror groups. As Charles Perrow argues that in complex systems like nuclear facilities, security must be more reliable and tightly regulated. Focusing on the people providing physical security to these facilities, it is important to be cognizant of the fact that many a time, it is a situation where very bright people are engaged in very boring jobs. This is a recipe for disaster as brought out in the Y-12 National Security Complex at Oak Ridge, Tennessee and more recently in the case of cheating by US missile officers in their proficiency tests. Thus it is important to ensure that the first responders or the personnel guarding these facilities are constantly motivated, their training is upgraded and morale is high.

Given the existence of large amounts of fissile material across the globe, several successful cases of unauthorised access by activist groups to weapons and fissile material storage facilities and the stated intent of terror groups like the Al Qaeda, the absence of a nuclear terrorism incident is quite puzzling. We can ascribe it to either pure luck or successful thwarting of such attempts by security and police forces. However, nuclear terrorism is a danger that is very real and which we must collectively guard against.

NOTES

1 Arun Vishwanathan is Associate Professor, Centre for Security Studies, School of National Security Studies, Central University of Gujarat, INDIA. An earlier version of this paper was published in *International Journal for Social Science Research and Global Security*, Vol. 1 (1), January-March 2018. The author can be reached at arun_summerhill@yahoo.com

2 Pierluigi Paganini, "ISIS use of Telegram has definitively surpassed Twitter", *Security Affairs*, December 27, 2016, http://securityaffairs.co/wordpress/54787/terrorism/telegram-isis.html

3 "Testimony by Jawal al-Fadl in United States v. Usama bin Laden", US District Court Southern District of New York. Judge Leonard B. Sand, February 6, 2001, pp. 35-41, 153-54, 363, cited in Rolf Mowatt-Larsenn, *Al Qaeda Weapons of Mass Destruction: Hype or Reality*, Cambridge: Belfer Center for Science and International Affairs, January 2010, pp. 11-12.

4 Rolf Mowatt-Larsenn, "Al Qaeda's Nuclear Ambitions", *Foreign Policy*, November 16, 2010, http://foreignpolicy.com/2010/11/16/al-qaedas-nuclear-ambitions/

5 Feroz Hassan Khan and Emily Burke, "Tackling Nuclear Terrorism in South Asia", *Prism*, Vol. 5, No. 1, pp. 84-85.

6 "IAEA Incident and Trafficking Database (ITDB): Incidents of nuclear and other radioactive material out of regulatory control, 2016 Factsheet", International Atomic Energy Agency, December 2015, https://www-ns.iaea.org/downloads/security/itdb-fact-sheet.pdf

7 "IAEA Incident and Trafficking Database (ITDB) 2004", International Atomic Energy Agency, December 2004, http://www.nuclearfiles.org/menu/key-issues/nuclear-weapons/issues/governance/iaea/PDFs/itdb_31122004[1].pdf

8 List of incidents compiled from "IAEA Incident and Trafficking Database (ITDB) 2004", International Atomic Energy Agency, December 2004, http://www.nuclearfiles.org/menu/key-issues/nuclear-weapons/issues/governance/iaea/PDFs/itdb_31122004[1].pdf

9 Paul Leventhal and Brahma Chellaney, "Nuclear Terrorism: Threat, Perception and Response in South Asia", Presentation at the Institute for Defence Studies and Analyses, October 10, 1988, New Delhi.

10 International Panel on Fissile Materials, "Global Fissile Material Report 2015: Nuclear Weapon and Fissile Material Stockpiles and Production", 2015, p. 2.

11 "The Database on Nuclear Power Reactors", Power Reactor Information System, *International Atomic Energy Agency*, https://www.iaea.org/pris/

12 "Reactors Under Construction", Power Reactor Information System, *International Atomic Energy Agency*, https://www.iaea.org/PRIS/WorldStatistics/UnderConstruction ReactorsByCountry.aspx

13 Eric Schlosser, "Break in At Y-12", *The New Yorker*, March 9, 2015, http://www.newyorker.com/magazine/2015/03/09/break-in-at-y-12

14 To read in detail about the entire break-in of the y-12 facility see, Dan Zak, "The Prophets of Oak Ridge", April 30, 2013, *Washington Post*, http://www.washingtonpost.com/sf/wp-style/2013/09/13/the-prophets-of-oak-ridge/

15 Eric Schlosser, "Break in At Y-12", The New Yorker, March 9, 2015, http://www.newyorker.com/magazine/2015/03/09/break-in-at-y-12

16 Charles Perrow, "Fukushima, risk, and probability: Expect the unexpected", *Bulletin of Atomic Scientists*, April 1, 2011, http://thebulletin.org/fukushima-risk-and-probability-expect-unexpected-0

17 P.R. Chari, "India's Role in the Hague Nuclear Security Summit", *Carnegie Endowment for International Peace*, March 18, 2014, http://carnegieendowment.org/2014/03/18/india-s-role-in-hague-nuclear-security-summit/h4iw

18 "NTI Nuclear Security Index", *Nuclear Threat Initiative*, January 2016, http://ntiindex.org/wp-content/uploads/2016/03/NTI_2016-Index-Report_MAR-25-2.pdf

19 Patrick Takahashi, "Why Worry About Fukushima When Hiroshima and Nagasaki Are Safe?" *Huffington Post*, http://www.huffingtonpost.com/patrick-takahashi/why-worry-about-fukushima_b_847250.html; "Fukushima caesium leaks 'equal 168 Hiroshimas'", *The Telegraph*, August 25, 2011, http://www.telegraph.co.uk/news/worldnews/asia/japan/8722400/Fukushima-caesium-leaks-equal-168-Hiroshimas.html

20 Shaun Gregory, "The Terrorist Threat To Pakistan's Nuclear Weapons", *CTC Sentinel*, Vol. 2, No. 7, July 2009, https://www.ctc.usma.edu/v2/wp-content/uploads/2010/06/Vol2Iss7-Art1.pdf

11

Military Diplomacy: Analysis of the Chinese Model and Lessons for India

Brig. Madhusudan R. Mutatkar

"There is a theory that China will tend to push, and if you bend, they will push some more."

—Benigno Aquino III Outgoing President of Philippines,
Time 06 Jun 2016

Introduction

In the realm of national strategic considerations, one finds that military and diplomatic affairs merge in an intertwining relationship. At this point, it must be recognised that diplomacy and military force are inseparable instruments of national policy. Except in those international agreements, which contain automatic sanctions, the only guarantee by which a treaty may be kept in force is the actual or implied threat of retaliatory action. The threat of the force of arms is the ultimate sanction, which supports any diplomatic action. Diplomacy, which depends upon only political or economic sanctions, rests upon a precarious base; diplomacy unsupported by a force in being has the appearance of a bluff. Chamberlain's attempts at appeasement of Hitler failed miserably in the Second World War, since it lacked the required force. For this reason, the military capability to exert the force of arms in the appropriate place is essential in support of successful diplomacy. Conversely, diplomatic action can contribute importantly to the achievement of military capability.[2]

On the face of it, military and diplomacy seem to belong to two very different realms. Diplomacy is peaceful interaction between nations aimed at resolving differences and promoting cooperation. If diplomacy is the first line of engagement between states, military is seen as the last and involves use of force. The connection between diplomacy and use of force, however, should not be seen as two ends of a spectrum. States have long used demonstration of military capabilities and threats of use of force as instruments to boost negotiating leverage with other states. Gunboat diplomacy is a well-known tactic used in modern statecraft.[3]

China uses military diplomacy extensively and calls it "foreign affairs work performed by defence institutions and armed forces." With the greater use of military diplomacy we can enhance the pursuit of a country's national interest.[4]

Ideology and Strategy

From the earliest days of history, many of the great minds of warfare addressed the need to understand the inevitable influence and involvement of military activities in affairs outside of war fighting. The linkage between military activities and those of diplomacy, economics, information, intelligence, and other elements of national power is not a new found concept; rather it is a concept that dates back to centuries. From the earliest days of warfare, military theorists and practitioners, the likes of Sun Tzu, Frederick the Great, Carl von Clausewitz, and Alfred Thayer Mahan, recognised the interconnection between these elements and a need to coordinate and integrate them to achieve maximum effectiveness. These respected intellectuals have in their own ways established the need for understanding the role of military beyond the limits of pure warfare. Specifically the linkage of the military with diplomacy is undeniably the most prominent. A common notion among these theorists and practitioners is the effectiveness of advancing foreign policy utilising the military as a purveyor of diplomacy.[5]

In recent years there has been much interest in the qualities and characteristics that have made the Chinese approach to warfare different from that of other societies (especially the European and European-descended societies usually labeled as "the West"). Some authors, pointing to the Confucian tradition and certain passages in Sun Tzu's *Art of War*, have argued that China's traditional grand strategy has emphasised defence over offence and displayed a preference for non-violent solutions to security problems.

Sun Tzu, after all, tells us that the acme of military excellence is to subdue the enemy without fighting, while the *Mencius*, one of the core texts of the Confucian canon, maintains that the truly virtuous ruler, by means of his transforming influence, can bring his enemies to submit voluntarily without recourse to physical coercion. Others, most notably the Western military historian John Keegan, have argued that China has followed an "Oriental" style of war-making characterised by caution, delay, and the avoidance of battle, and use of elaborate ruses and stratagems; this style of Warfare is contrasted with a "Western way of war" that stresses direct, face-to-face confrontation and the rapid resolution of military conflicts by the main force.[6]

In the chapter on "Attack by Stratagem", Sun Tzu explains, "To fight and conquer in all your battles is not supreme excellence; supreme excellence consists in breaking the enemy's resistance without fighting." Further explaining the futility of war he elaborates "the skillful leader subdues the enemy's troops without fighting; he captures their cities without laying siege to them; he overthrows their kingdom without lengthy operations in the field. With his forces intact he will dispute the mastery of the empire, and thus, without losing a man, his triumph will be complete. This is the method of attacking by stratagem."[7]

The growing importance of diplomacy was very evident in the recent example of the Indo-China face-off at Dokalam (Dolam) plateau. Though the two countries' militaries were in an eyeball-to-eyeball confrontation also involving some "pushing and shoving" by the ground troops and also the Chinese side hinting and reminding of lessons of 1962 conflict—but perceptibly, all over, the call was to try and resolve the impasse diplomatically; and finally the matter was resolved without firing a single shot. What is debatable is that was it military diplomacy or was it overall foreign policy or a combination of both, which finally did the trick.

Military Diplomacy in China's Context

Military is only one part of the overall policy making community in China, and China is not a military-controlled country. They have a civilian culture with civilian control over the military.

At a meeting that took place in Beijing in January 2015, Chinese President and Chairman of the Central Military Commission Xi Jinping called upon People's Liberation Army (PLA) officers to start "a new phase of military diplomacy." The PLA's increasing willingness to participate in joint exercises with other nations allows the PLA to showcase the new capabilities that have resulted from its modernisation and helps the PLA maintain its security interests in the region and around the world. Given President Xi's exhortation for greater PLA foreign relations to realise the "Chinese Dream" that includes making China "a stronger nation with a strong military", we can expect to see the PLA continue participating in bilateral and multilateral joint exercises with foreign militaries in the future.[8]

Chinese Definition of Military Diplomacy[9]

Chinese definitions of military diplomacy are broad and encompass a wide variety of activities. A 2007 book by the PLA National Defence University (NDU) Strategy Teaching and Research Department defines military diplomacy as "diplomatic activities that are carried out by countries in the realm of military affairs, in service of national defence or military strategy." A more recent definition in the 2011 edition of PLA Military Terminology characterises military diplomacy as:

> External relationships pertaining to military and related affairs between countries and groups of countries, including military personnel exchange, military negotiations, arm control negotiations, military aid, military intelligence cooperation, military technology cooperation, international peacekeeping, military alliance activities, etc. Military diplomacy is an important component of a country's foreign relations.

PLA scholars consider a coherent military diplomacy strategy a "necessary part of the national interest", arguing that military relations can "serve as a planning construct for national strategy.... contain actual or perceived enemies...and spur national military construction. The spectrum of military diplomatic activities is broad, including "military alliances, strategic dialogues, trust-building measures, military negotiations, military intelligence exchanges, military technical cooperation, international military work, border cooperation, international military personnel training, military support activities, military trade, and military academic exchanges."

PLA academicians have ascribed a variety of functions to military diplomacy, drawing distinctions between peacetime, wartime, and crisis functions.

Peace-Time: During peacetime, military diplomacy "maintains and develops bilateral military security relations...provides a platform for handling international security issues...molds the country's military...and promotes national defence and military construction.

War-Time: In time of war, military diplomacy serves to "strengthen our alliances and weaken those of the enemy...win military aid and material support for combat....win international moral and legal support....provide a channel to end the war....and resolve post-war problems."

Crisis-Time: Crisis applications of military diplomacy include preventing and reducing crisis, along with creating, facing, and intensifying crisis when necessary or beneficial.

Chinese military diplomatic activities largely conform to the PLA's peacetime conceptions of military diplomacy. Stated objectives are derived from broader PLA missions and include supporting overall national foreign policy, protecting national sovereignty, advancing national interests, and shaping the international security environment. Xi Jinping cited several goals for Chinese military diplomacy in the January 2015 speech to the All-Military Diplomatic Work Conference, including supporting overall national foreign policy, and protecting national security. Xi also highlighted the goals of protecting China's sovereignty, security, and development interests. Academics and scholars have further added the following as the goals and objectives of military diplomacy:

(a) Support overall national foreign policy and the new era of military strategic direction.

(b) Shape the international security environment and promote military modernisation.

(c) Ensure national sovereignty and territorial integrity, promote Chinese military reform, build advantageous international military relations, and safeguard world peace and stability.

Some other goals of military diplomacy include: intelligence gathering, learning new skills and benchmarking PLA capabilities against those of other nations, building partner capacity, and promoting sales of Chinese weapons—these goals of military diplomacy though typically omitted or only mentioned briefly in the Chinese official documents are implicit.

Much of the PLA's current military diplomatic activity is focused on protecting and advancing specific Chinese strategic interests. Chinese foreign policy emphasises managing strategic relations with great powers such as USA and Russia and engaging countries on China's periphery and APEC members. China is increasingly dependent on oil and natural gas imported from Middle East and Africa; the PLA Navy's (PLAN) counter-piracy presence in the Gulf of Aden facilitates strategic ties in the Middle East and Africa, helps guarantee China's energy security, and provides operational experience in protecting China's sea lines of communication. Xi Jinping's signature foreign policy contribution is the Belt and Road initiative; PLA interactions with militaries in Europe, Africa, Central Asia, and South Asia reinforce this effort.

Strategic Vs Operational Objectives

Chinese military diplomacy objectives can be divided into strategic and operational categories. Strategic objectives include supporting overall PRC diplomacy by engaging key countries and providing public goods and shaping the security environment by displaying or deploying PLA capabilities. Operational goals are intended to improve the PLA's ability to fight and win wars; these include collecting intelligence on foreign military capabilities and intentions and on potential operating areas, and learning new skills and tactics, techniques and procedures from other militaries.

Supporting PRC Diplomacy

Military diplomacy supports broader Chinese diplomatic efforts by engaging key countries and undertaking all possible activities, which help to enhance China's image. Chinese writings strongly emphasise the PLA's obedience to the Chinese Communist Party (CCP) and by extension view military diplomacy as a tool used to advance larger CCP foreign policy goals. Top-down implementation of Chinese military diplomacy and the broad parameters of this objective means that nearly all military diplomatic activities are intended to advance wider Chinese diplomatic goals. Senior-level meetings, strategic dialogues, and functional exchanges are often used to deliver diplomatic talking points, non-traditional security operations provide public goods that enhance China's international reputation, and military exercises are often presented as examples of international co-operation.

Shaping the Security Environment

Military diplomacy will also involve deployment and/or display of PLA capabilities to shape the security environment. The 2015 Defence White Paper calls on the PLA to develop military to military relations...and create a security environment favourable to China's peaceful development. Chinese scholars state that shaping a favourable security environment is a crucial mission of military diplomacy, and Chinese media often trumpet the display of PLA capabilities in the defence of national interests. Sino-Russian military exercises in the Mediterranean Sea and South China Sea are intended to show that the USA and countries in the Asia-Pacific region should take the strategic partnership between the two countries seriously.

Collecting Intelligence

Military diplomacy offers opportunities to collect intelligence on foreign capabilities and intentions, and on potential operating areas. Chinese sources do not openly mention intelligence gathering as an objective, but Chinese scholars explicitly warn against revealing secret information during military diplomatic exchanges, a tacit acknowledgment of the intelligence potential of military diplomacy. Nearly all military diplomatic activities can be employed to gather some kind of intelligence because military diplomacy by definition provides some degree of access to foreign militaries. Senior level meetings and dialogues provide opportunities to collect political intelligence about policy preferences and personnel intelligence about foreign military leaders, functional exchanges and military exercises offer technical intelligence about foreign military capabilities, and naval port calls and non-traditional security operations can be used to collect intelligence about potential operating areas.

Learning New Skills, Tactics, Techniques and Procedures

Military diplomacy allows the PLA to learn new skills from other countries and benchmark PLA capabilities against those of other nations. Chinese defence white papers consistently emphasise learning from other militaries as a goal of military diplomacy, and quasi-official Chinese sources stress the importance of learning new skills and benchmarking PLA capabilities against those of foreign nations. Chinese scholars emphasise the value of exercises for practising military skills, and military exercises with foreign partners allow the PLA to compare its capabilities and learn from foreign militaries. Examples include PLA Air Force (PLAAF) participation in Russia's multilateral Aviadarts 2014 competition, while Chinese participation in the 2005 Peace Mission exercise helped the PLA learn new skills, with PLAAF fighters refueling from Russian aerial tankers for the first time.

The USA emphasises the importance of military diplomacy and arms sales in building the capacity of allies and partners and in improving the US military's ability to operate with them in combined and coalition operations. Authoritative Chinese sources do not cite building partner capacity as a goal, but PLA writings identify military aid as an important function of military diplomacy that encompasses the transfers of "weapons, military supplies, technology, and expertise" that can "strengthen political, military, and economic relations between countries." The PLA appears to view building partner capacity as a means of strengthening bilateral relations rather than as an end in itself. Today's more capable PLA has more to teach less-advanced militaries. Prominent examples of Chinese military diplomacy that were meant to build partner capacity include the Sino-Pakistani Shaheen exercises and Chinese military aid to Afghanistan. Chinese writings do not stress building interoperability with partners as an explicit goal of military diplomacy, but this theme is evident in recent combined exercises with Russia.

Three-War Strategy—Military Diplomacy

Although China has not been involved in any military campaigns since 1979, China continues to lay claims on territories and islands in South China Sea, Arunachal Pradesh, Bhutan, etc. The Chinese military has an important role in this context; Chinese military has been actively involved on the military diplomatic front. China has also been expanding its influence in various parts of the world by various projects—the latest being the Belt & Road Initiative. These initiatives seem to be reviving the "Middle Kingdom" concept in a very subtle and inconspicuous way.[10] Dr Michael Raska in an article in *The Diplomat*, December 2015, has explained this very concept as—"The Three Warfare Strategy". In 2003, the Central Military Commission (CMC) approved the guiding conceptual umbrella for information operations for the People's Liberation Army (PLA)—the "Three Warfares" (*san zhongzhanfa*). The concept is based on three mutually reinforcing strategies:

(a) the coordinated use of strategic psychological operations;
(b) overt & covert media manipulation; and
(c) legal warfare designed to manipulate strategies, defence policies, and perceptions of target audiences abroad.

Operationalising the "Three Warfares"

At the Operational level, the "Three Warfares" became the responsibility for the PLA's General Political Department's Liaison Department (GPD/LD), which conducts diverse political, financial, military, and intelligence operations. GPD/LD consists of four bureaus:

(a) A liaison bureau responsible for clandestine Taiwan-focused operations;

(b) An investigation and research bureau responsible for international security analysis and friendly contact;

(c) An external propaganda bureau responsible for disintegration operations, including psychological operations, development of propaganda themes, and legal analysis; and

(d) A border defence bureau responsible for managing border negotiations and agreements.

In practice, the GPD/LD is also linked with the PLA General Staff Department (GSD) 2nd department led intelligence network. One of its core activities is identifying select foreign political, business, and military elites and organisations abroad relevant to China's interests or potential 'friendly contacts'. The GPD/LD investigation and research bureau then analyses their position towards China, career trajectories, motivations, political orientations, factional affiliations, and competencies.

The resultant "cognitive maps" guide the direction and character of tailored influence operations, including conversion, exploitation, or subversion. Meanwhile, the GPD's Propaganda Department broadcasts sustained internal and external strategic perception management campaigns through mass media and cyberspace channels to promote specific themes favourable for China's image abroad—political stability, peace, ethnic harmony, and economic prosperity supporting the narrative of the "China model" (*zhongguo moshi*). The exploitation of such information operations represents Beijing's hybrid or "non-kinetic" attempts to direct influence in strategic areas of competition in Asia and Europe.[11]

Three-Warfare Strategies – Asian Context

In the Asian context China is probably using the Three-Warfare Strategy to wrest its "claimed territories"; Doklam (Dolam) was probably one of the latest example. The other such example is of South China Sea. China claims nearly all of the South China Sea as its own through maps marked with a U-shaped, nine dash line that dates from 1947. China has been adept at producing maps and quoting historical precedents to build a legal argument and its media offensive has backed it up regularly.

Case Study: Philippines. In 2013, the Philippines government filed a case with a UN tribunal at Hague arguing against Beijing's South China Sea claims.[12] In 2016 the UNCLOS tribunal ruled against China dismissing its claims in South China Sea. Though Philippines achieved a major international victory against a more powerful neighbour, China, with its application of the Three Warfares, successfully "co-opted" its president, Rodrigo Duterte, after he assumed office in 2016. Beijing also successfully played on his animosity to former US President Obama. A year later, China has emerged victorious, nobody mentions the UNCLOS ruling and Philippines have submitted to Beijing.[13]

Re-organisation of the Chinese Army

A major indicator of China's resolve at military diplomacy is the recent military re-organisation. As part of the re-organisation in early 2016 major changes to the PLA's structure were instituted, including the creation of 15 organisations under the CMC. Specifically, the former General Staff Department is now the CMC Joint Staff Department, the former General Political Department is the CMC Political Work Department, the former General Logistics Department is the CMC Logistics Support Department, and the former General Armament Department is the Equipment Development Department. The PLA Army also created a separate PLA Army (PLAA) Headquarters; renamed the Second Artillery Force as the PLA Rocket Force and upgraded it from an independent branch to a full service, and created five Theatre Commands from the previous seven Military Regions.

The 2016 re-organisation also placed the office with primary responsibility for coordinating PLA foreign relations (the Ministry of National Defence – Foreign Affairs Office) under the direct supervision of the CMC and renamed it the CMC Office of International Military Cooperation, possibly reflecting Xi Jinping's heightened emphasis on military diplomacy.[14]

Indian Perspective

There are a number of lessons for India from the aforementioned Chinese model. Historically Kautilya's *Arthashastra* has also propagated the use of "*mantra yudh*", i.e. diplomatic offensive—particularly in the context of attacks in the rear and while dealing with weak kings. As elucidated by L N Rangarajan in the translation of the *Arthashastra*, war in the context of foreign policy includes everything, from undertaking a diplomatic offensive to fighting a battle.[15]

Military diplomacy occupies little space in the public imagination in India. India needs to leverage the awesome reputation its peacekeepers have built across the wide spectrum of countries in the world. Indian diplomatic efforts need a major boost. India has conducted successful military diplomacy right from its independence. The sterling actions by our troops deployed for peace-keeping operations in Korea, Congo, Somalia to name a few and the contribution to the training of foreign armies of Bhutan, Lesotho, Zambia, Laos Nepal, Sri Lanka and US are well known.[16] The Indian military diplomatic efforts can be enhanced by more frequent and larger participation in international training programmes, exercises and peacekeeping missions. Other activities like military conferences, joint border interactions/meetings, joint maritime patrols and surveillance, joint humanitarian assistance and disaster relief, seminars, symposia on military subjects, military sports events, adventure activities and institutional cooperation between think tanks like IDSA, CLAWS, and USI will help enhance Indian diplomatic efforts. Some other aspects which merit attention on the operational front are India's vast experience in mountain warfare (Siachin is the highest battlefield in the world), counter-insurgency and jungle warfare which can be leveraged towards building cooperation and showcasing our superior capabilities. All such actions towards overall building of a robust foreign policy will also go a long way in increasing our military and diplomatic outreach and preparing the country's strategic awareness.

India has to maintain mutually beneficiary relationships with less than 200 nation states. India has roughly 900 diplomats staffing 120 embassies and 49 consulates. In a stark contrast USA has over 20,000, UK 6,000 and China 4,200. As far as the number of diplomats is concerned Indian numbers are comparable only to countries like Singapore and New Zealand.[17] Notwithstanding the fact that there is a shortage of qualified and trained professionals for diplomatic missions, a beginning can be made—cross posting of Armed Forces officers (who have training in studying capabilities of other countries) can be an excellent start. Also Armed Forces officers on deputation to the Ministry of External Affairs can make a positive difference. The "Deliberations of a Working Group on Military and Diplomacy"[18] in 2013 has given concrete recommendations on enhancing the country's diplomatic efforts—however these need to be implemented.

Conclusion

Pursuance of national interest as a foreign policy goal is the primary justification for all kinds of state actions. Capabilities take time to build up but intentions may change overnight. The Chinese are known to use guile and stratagem to hide their intentions and build capabilities to strike (or threaten to strike) at the time and place of their choice. India through an extremely balanced approach and astute diplomacy successfully defused the situation in Doklam. The Chinese bullying tactics were neither the first nor the last instance. To build our capabilities and be capable of countering any future machinations, enhancing our diplomatic reach has now become an extremely important national security imperative, which needs utmost priority at all levels. As per C. Raja Mohan in the *Indian Express* of 08 December 2010, "*While the civilian bureaucracy and the political leadership in our Ministry of Defence (MoD) continue to constrain the Indian military's engagement with the world, China is consciously promoting it.*"[19] It is high time we not only learn our lessons but also start acting on them.

NOTES

1 Big stick ideology, big stick diplomacy refers to US President Theodore Roosevelt's foreign policy: "speak softly, and carry a big stick." The idea of negotiating peacefully, simultaneously threatening with the "big stick", or the military, ties in heavily with the idea of Realpolitik, which implies a pursuit of political power that resembles Machiavellian ideals. It is comparable to gunboat diplomacy, as used in international politics by imperial powers. https://en.wikipedia.org/wiki/Big_Stick_ideology

2 Military Geography—Louis C Peltier and G Etzel Pearcy, 1966, p. 9

3 C. Raja Mohan in National University of Singapore, ISAS Working Paper No. 144, 20 February 2012

4 India's Military Conflicts and Diplomacy, Gen VP Malik, 2013, p. 180

5 Military Diplomacy : An Essential Tool of Foreign Policy at the Theatre Strategic Level, By Major James E. Willard, US Army, 25 May 2006.

6 A Military History of China, Ed by David A Graff & Robin Higham, pp 12-13

7 Major James E. Willard, US Army, ibid

8 The Huffington Post, in association with the Times of India Group 12 April 2015

9 China Strategic Perspective 11—Centre for the Study of Chinese Military Affairs, Institute for National Strategic Studies, National Defence University, Washington DC July 2017.

10 Historically China has considered itself to be the Middle Kingdom and all other states on its periphery as vassals who would pay tribute. On studying the series of White Papers published since 1998 to 2014 the "Middle Kingdom Context" seems to be re-surfacing, albeit in a very subtle and soft way.

11 Three War Strategy :Practising Military Diplomacy Michael Raska, 18 Dec 2015, *The Diplomat.*

12 Hannah Beech, *The Time*, "Welcome to South China Sea"; 06 June 2016.

13 IndraniBagchi, *Times of India Group*, 13 Aug 2017

14 China Strategic Perspective 11, ibid, p. 7

15 L.N. Rangarajan, Kautilya, *The Arthashastra*, Penguin books, 1992, p. 513

16 Brig KA Muthanna, Perspectives Military Diplomacy, https//www.idsa.in.jds_5_ 1_ kamuthanna

17 Brig A K Pattanaik in 'Military Diplomacy: Strengthening Linkages in India's Neighbourhood', Scholar Warrior, Spring 2016

18 Institute of Defence Studies and Analysis, 2013 at http://www.idsa.in

19 Lt Gen Aditya Singh (Retd), Synergising Defence and Diplomacy, Issue brief, Delhi Policy Group, September 2015

Index